Get A Grip

Growing Recurring Income Potential

RAY ROBBINS

with **Kevin Robbins**

Get A Grip

This publication is designed to provide general information regarding the subject matter covered. However, laws and practices often vary from state to state and are subject to change. Because each factual situation is different, specific advice should be tailored to the particular circumstances. For this reason, the reader is advised to consult with his or her own advisor regarding each specific situation.

The author and publisher have taken reasonable precautions in the preparation of this book and believe the facts presented within are accurate as of the date it was written. However, neither the author nor the publisher assumes any responsibility for any errors or omissions. The author and publisher specifically disclaim any liability resulting from the use or application of the information contained in this book, and the information is not intended to serve as legal, financial, or other professional advice related to individual situations.

Published by Lazy River Publishing
For ordering information or special discounts for bulk purchases, please contact:
www.mannamotion.com

Cover design and composition by Accelerate Media Partners, LLC
Copy editing by The Media Concierge, LLC

Paperback ISBN: 978-0-692-09081-7
Library of Congress Control Number: 2018903254

BUS025000 BUSINESS & ECONOMICS / Entrepreneurship
Printed in the United States of America

Dedication

· ◆ ·

This book is dedicated to the many trainers and teachers in the network marketing industry whose driving force is to lift others up by showing them how to be in business for themselves, how to become professional presenters, and how to teach and grow other leaders.

I also dedicate this writing to God, my family, and the many friends I have in the industry. They are the why that motivates me every day.

CONTENTS

• ◆ •

FOREWORD

• ◆ •

I grew up in a family where my dad was always bigger than life. Attitude was 95 percent of every equation. If you had the right attitude, anything was possible.

One of the first stories I remember Dad telling me was how he used his incredible attitude to win my mom over. Dad was in the Army when he first met my mom. He was training to serve in Vietnam as a helicopter pilot. You might think that heading to fight a dangerous war wouldn't have given Dad much leverage to ask a girl to marry him, but then you don't know my dad. Dad soon won Mom's heart. The toughest part of the courtship was convincing my grandparents that an ambitious but poor, skinny kid from Texas, who was on his way to war would be able to provide a great life for their daughter. When Dad met with my grandfather for the first time, he knew that even though the conversation would be tough, he would win my mom's family over. He promised he'd always take care of my mom and then he boldy promised that he would never make less than $1,000 a month, a salary Dad believed would provide a great life for my mom.

I'd say my dad under promised and over delivered. Today, Dad is one of the top ten money earners of all time in the network marketing industry. Dad knew he could do anything he set his mind to and he made his point! That 95 percent has gotten Dad everything he has in his life—his wife, his family, his business—everything.

Dad has found success in many different endeavors from selling women's pantyhose, to selling children's books, to selling some of the first video game machines, like Pac-Man and Space Invaders, but for Dad, the "what" has never been as important as the "why." His success came because his attitude is that he can *make* things happen. He calls this forcing the issue. Dad believes in his success long before he ever has any tangible evidence that it will come. He also has a passion for connecting with people. Having a positive attitude and connecting people is the secret to his success.

When Dad walks into a restaurant, he often introduces himself to strangers. He might even sit down with them and have a bite of dessert. Within moments, strangers feel like they're visiting with an old friend. This may seem strange to you and I, but Dad does this every day.

Dad's interest in meeting new people is an extension of his desire to help encourage and lift people up. He truly believes that through network marketing, he can improve their lives. This attitude has become his legacy. As a result, he's helped thousands of people, including me, make extra income, pay off debts, start college funds, save for that exotic vacation, and start full time careers.

More than twenty years ago, Dad encouraged me to start my own network marketing business. Believe it or not, I didn't want to do it. I had a college degree and was relatively successful in my corporate job where I was an outside sales representative for a temporary job placement company. In fact, I was just too busy to think about starting a business. Besides, my personality isn't quite like my dad's. I thought you had to be like Ray Robbins to be successful. I thought you had to have the type of personality that loved walking into a room or a restaurant and immediately meeting everyone in it. I'm not wired that way.

Basically, I had a lot of excuses for *not* getting started in network marketing. What I had, was the wrong *attitude* for success. Instead of believing in my own future success, I believed that I wouldn't be successful. I know there are people out there that share this attitude. Maybe you're one of them. Maybe someone you've talked to about network marketing has this attitude.

The good news is that there are plenty of people out there who have the right attitude toward success and are actively looking for ways to make extra income. You simply have to find them. Many of us can even eventually change our attitude toward success. I know I did.

My dad helped me develop the right attitude for success and now he wants to help you do the same. Are you just starting out in network marketing? Are you trying to decide if this business is right for you? Maybe you feel stuck in your current job. Wherever you are, *Get A Grip* was written for you. By the time you finish reading *Get A Grip*, you'll understand why Dad chose to put his energy in network marketing and why he continues helping others in this business.

My dad would have succeeded in any business in any industry. He chose to succeed in network marketing because it's one industry where he could completely invest himself in helping others lift themselves up. First, Dad developed a successful attitude. Then he put that attitude toward his passion. Only then did he have numerous successes. Now, he wants to share the lessons he's learned with you so that you can create your own story of success.

If you have the right attitude, you can achieve anything. *Get A Grip* will show you how network marketing can help you do that.

Kevin Robbins

LETTER FROM THE AUTHOR

• ◆ •

I love this industry. I love the fact that anyone can do it. I love hearing how it has helped countless people lift themselves out of debt to find significant financial success. I love hearing stories about the people who have created their own business—with purpose—from home.

This industry has many great companies that offer high-quality products and a realistic opportunity for success. However, like any other industry, there are also some not-so-great companies that are built on substandard products and lots of hype.

The network marketing industry is currently going through some changes that will allow those great companies to stand out. I believe this is a good thing. When products are over-hyped, or when people are told network marketing is a get-rich-quick business, it ultimately hurts everyone. Customers want to buy a product or service that has value. They also want to buy a product or service that can improve their quality of life or solve a problem. As with any business, the equation for success is simple: product value = more customers = more income.

PRODUCT VALUE =
MORE CUSTOMERS =
MORE INCOME

When a company offers a product of value, a business opportunity is created for distributors who can offer that value to customers. Leverage is achieved in network marketing by finding other distributors who can offer that product value to customers. Again, when a good product or service is offered, the equation for success is simple: product value = more customers = more income.

There was a time when people who were new to the industry were taught that the only way to be successful was to find other people who wanted to make money. They were also promised big money, lavish lifestyles, and over-the-top riches for what seemed like little or no real effort.

The idea was that the person would find four other people who wanted to make money who would then find four more people who wanted to make money and so on and so forth. The math always worked. The money was always so easily attained, but that pitch left out two important factors:

First, the product. The product or service in the above example became incidental. In today's world, the product is never incidental. Companies that fail to focus on the quality of their products, companies that fail to deliver real product benefits, and companies that fail to ultimately market to real customers *will* find themselves lagging behind.

Second, it's equally important to understand that not every person who joins this industry goes on to become a huge money earner with a lavish lifestyle. If that is the only focus, it can be misleading. Far more people find success in this business earning part-time income. Plus, as you will learn in this book, network marketing takes effort, real work. But as you will also find out that part time income can be very rewarding. I think it can dramatically improve someone's financial outlook. Are there opportunities beyond the part-time income? Of course! There are stories in this book of people who have been tremendously blessed, but I also like to highlight the successes of many thousands of people that participate in this business every day to earn extra money to help pay their bills, pay off some debt, or earn a little extra spending money. Those are real success stories, too.

In summary, of course I believe in making money, in finding other people who are interested in making money, and in creating leverage. In fact, I believe the network marketing industry is on the cusp of having huge growth over the next decade. But I also believe that in order to make money and create leverage in this industry, *everything* has to be based on the customers who buy the product or service. When that happens, the opportunity to earn income is legitimate, substantial and, for those who desire it, recurring.

Fortunately, I learned the value of focusing on customers long before I went into network marketing. I learned to focus on them when I was in the education, retail, vending, and food industries. Why? Because no matter what industry you're in, the only way to make money is to keep your customers happy. Happy customers will buy your product over and over again. Happy customers will also give you referrals, thus bringing you more customers.

Thank you for giving me the opportunity to show how network marketing can help you get a grip and change your life.

Sincerely,

Ray Robbins

INTRODUCTION

· ◆ ·

"Some people want it to happen, some people wish it would happen, others make it happen."

—Michael Jordon

When I was a young man growing up in San Antonio, Texas, I knew I was different from the rest of my family. I didn't think like them. When my parents started sentences with, "We can't afford . . ." I didn't understand why not. I found it confusing. It didn't take long before I started wondering if other families said the same thing. I started asking questions like, "Why can't we afford things when so many other families can?" I was a thorn in my parents' side. However, once I realized that this question hurt their feelings, I backed off, but that question opened my mind to hear what other people who didn't say, "I can't afford," were doing.

Near our house, there was a donut shop where I spent a lot of time. One day during the shop's slow season, I was eating a donut and asking the owner some questions—I was always asking questions—and he said, "You're an enterprising little guy, aren't you? You know what? God gave you a gift, and you need to go into business for yourself. You're an entrepreneur."

I come from a long line of farmers who never had any money. I didn't know what that guy was talking about, but I listened.

"Do you know what consignment is?" he asked.

I didn't, but he explained consignment and the act of delivering goods to others in terms I could understand.

"I'll consign you a dozen donuts," he said. "You walk out of here without paying me. Then you go out there and people buy these donuts for $0.10 each. When you come back, I'll only charge you $0.05 for every donut sold."

Well that was all I had to hear. I left that store like a shot and I sold those donuts. Then I sold a dozen more. Before I knew it, I had my own business.

Those first few donuts soon turned into hundreds of donuts. Before long, I was walking all over the place selling donuts. I knew which one of my customers wanted what. I knew that every Wednesday, Doctor Washer wanted a dozen chocolate glazed donuts and that Mr. McVries wanted a glazed donut with sprinkles.

In those days, selling a dozen donuts was a $0.60 profit for me, which was huge. The other kids started seeing what I was doing and asked to join, so I let them. I would take the neighborhood kids around, show them how to sell the donuts, and when I thought they were ready to go on their own, I'd take them to the donut shop owner and vouch for them. By the time I was done selling donuts, I had several friends working with me.

The lessons I learned selling donuts—work hard, use your own initiative, help others, and be gung ho about *everything*—have carried through to every business I've ever owned. When I got done selling those donuts, I had no choice but to start another business. Building businesses was—and still is—in my blood.

In high school, I started a lawnmowing business. I started it on my own with a single mower. By the time I graduated, I had many kids, including my best friends, working for me. I built that business just like I built the donut business. I found good people, trained them, and expanded my businesses by letting my employees work independently.

After high school, I went to junior college in San Antonio and then moved to Southwest Texas in San Marcos, which is now Texas State University, to study biology and chemistry. I was the first person in my family to finish college, so that was an important accomplishment for me. I thought I wanted to be a doctor, but when I moved to San Marcos, I just couldn't help but start another business. As soon as I arrived, I realized there wasn't a single place for kids to dance like there was in San Antonio. For me, that just wasn't good enough.

Even though San Marcos was a Baptist community, I started looking for a place to open a dance club. It wasn't something the community wanted, but I persevered. I found an old warehouse that looked like the Alamo, got a band to play on the upper level, and opened the Soul Hole. It was a dry community, so we were strict about making sure kids didn't sneak in alcohol. Let me tell you, the Soul Hole was a hit. Soon, even though we only opened on the weekends, I was making *a lot* of money. I'm not saying money is everything—it isn't and I'll get to that in a little bit—but making money gives you the freedom to help other people. The best way to make money is to get gung ho about whatever it is you're doing. When I sold donuts, I was gung ho about donuts. When I owned the Soul Hole, I was gung ho about the Soul Hole.

After graduating from college, I was drafted to go to Vietnam where I was a helicopter pilot and a commissioned officer. I loved being able to serve my country, but being in Vietnam was tough. However, from that experience, I learned some great lessons that I will share later in the book.

When I returned from Vietnam, I was gung ho about continuing my military career and becoming a general. Being gung ho means I'm all in and that attitude has done wonders for me.

I ended up going to a school that would set me on the path to becoming a general, but my wife, Dianna, wasn't quite as gung ho as I was about me being a general. She didn't want me shipping out to Asia again where I'd see more combat.

One of the problems with being gung ho is that sometimes you have to decide what to be gung ho about. I was gung ho about becoming a general, but I was also gung ho about being a good husband and making my wife happy. Although it wasn't an easy decision, I decided to stay in the states, which meant that professionally, I had to find something other than becoming a general to be gung ho about.

Before the war when I was in college, I'd thought about becoming a doctor, but when I returned from Vietnam, I was much more interested in going into business. I read a bunch of books about business and different industries and finally came across some information about the Montessori school movement, which was brand new at the time. Montessori was innovative because it let kids move through school at their own pace, which was a concept I absolutely loved. I knew that if I'd been in a system like that, I would have gotten through school two years earlier, so I got gung ho about Montessori.

The Montessori schools were having trouble getting funding for all the material they needed so I introduced them to Disney books, a line of classic books that were made to help kids become better readers and writers. Those books sold well, and before I knew it, I had them in many stores all over south Texas.

From there on, I jumped into any business I found interesting and that I thought could make money. Through the rest of the 1970s and the early 1980s, I got involved in a variety of businesses. I started a candle company to serve the many Catholics in San Antonio who use candles for religious purposes, and I worked for Frey Meats. Frey Meats was an interesting one. Tom Landry, who was head coach of the Dallas Cowboys at the time, had never publicly endorsed any product, but I helped him to do an ad with Frey Meats, which was a huge win for the company.

I also sold L'eggs pantyhose, which made me popular among my wife's friends. When I first started with Hanes, it was a fledgling company so they allowed us to choose a management training program that we wanted to go to that was put on by another company. I chose to go to the Xerox management training school and it was one of the most valuable trainings I've ever received.

In 1979, I started Robbins Vending. I was really interested in the new coin-operated video games that were popping up and thought they would become popular. I was right about that—the video gaming craze exploded a few years later—although plenty of people doubted that instinct at the time.

Not long after I started Robbins Vending, I went to a vending conference in New Orleans and came across the Pac-Man vendor. This is hard to believe now, but no one wanted to touch the product. They didn't like it and of the fifty games the vendor had at the conference, four were damaged. So, I talked the vendor down from $4,000 a machine to $2,000 each, bought all forty-six games, and brought them to Texas. I made a mistake though. I should have negotiated a deal to have an exclusive license with Pac-Man in Texas. If I'd done that, I would have made $10 million. But since I was the first to bring Pac-Man to our area, I still did really well. It was fun, too.

When video games became less popular, I started thinking about my next venture. Technically, I didn't have to go back to work for a while. I could have enjoyed the next ten to fifteen years just sitting around, but that's not my personality, so I looked at business opportunities here and there. Because I had done well, I had the luxury of being picky. Of the thousands of business opportunities out there, guess which one I picked?

Network marketing. I had years of business experience and had done well, yet network marketing was the number one business I wanted to get involved in. To me, it just made sense.

I started network marketing with a company that sold insulation material that, at the time, was used to protect rockets that were going into outer space. When a rocket goes into space, the sunny side is subject to 250 degrees Fahrenheit and the shaded side is subject to -250 degrees Fahrenheit. The insulation product provided a double-sided radiant barrier that could properly insulate both extremes. Turns out, this product was also great for insulating homes and was capable of vastly reducing home energy costs. At that time, no one other than NASA was using this product, but I believed in it, started selling it, and did well.

Remember, I didn't have to go back to work. I had experienced success with my other businesses and was simply curious. I wanted to see what other opportunities were out there. I went into network marketing because it intrigued me. I fell in love with it because it is *the* best way for anyone to make money. Wholesomeness, which I define as pursing greatness in everything—work, family, relationships, faith, charity—is far more important to me than money. However, one of my favorite quotes is, "There's nothing worse than a broke philanthropist."

If you want to save people's lives, you have to develop a lifestyle that will *help* other people. Think about that emergency procedure flight attendants walk through right before you take off. They tell you that in the case of an emergency, you put your oxygen mask over your face before you even think about helping someone else. If you don't put your mask on and you lose oxygen, you can't help anyone. The same goes for your personal finances. Helping yourself first empowers you to then help others. I know I've done it and it feels great.

Take this Washington state couple I know and love dearly. They bought a Cadillac for $36,000 with $5,000 down. After they signed the deal, the salesman said, "I'm really sorry, but I made a mistake. The car is actually $46,000."

The salesman felt bad about the mistake he'd made with the price and told them he'd honor the $36,000 price for twenty-four hours.

Like most people, these dear friends of mine had to secure outside financing for the remaining $31,000. They couldn't make it appear out of thin air, but they also couldn't get the money fast enough. I said, "Give me a minute," and I wired them $31,000.

As soon as they got the financing a few weeks later, they paid me back. So, they got the car for $10,000 less than the real cost of $46,000, and I was only out $31,000 for a few weeks. I tell this story because if I hadn't helped myself and my family first by getting my finances in order, I couldn't have helped these friends. Getting a grip over your finances gives you the freedom to live the life you want to live. It gives you the freedom to act charitably, and it gives you the freedom to help people.

You cannot help people if you aren't making a good living. Of the many industries in which I've served, network marketing is hands down the best way to do this. Network marketing gives you unlimited income potential with almost no overhead, research, or accounting . . . and very little investment.

Globally, the last ten years have been rough on many people. They've lost their homes due to foreclosure, and they've declared personal bankruptcy. Many of these hardships could have been avoided if the affected individuals had found a way to make a little more money. In many cases, a few hundred extra dollars a month might have prevented a personal bankruptcy or foreclosure. Unfortunately, these people lost their grip. I want to show you how to get a grip and keep it.

What does it mean to get a grip? Commonly, it means to settle down, take a survey of your current situation, realistically look at all the pros and cons in your life, and get your head out of the sand. It means to stop, pay attention, be silent, focus, and hold tight to what you know is right, good, wholesome, and productive so you can accentuate the positive and eliminate the negative. Getting a grip is often a shocking reminder that you might be ignoring important parts of your personal picture.

Once you start getting a grip, you can remove the detrimental, the weak, and the negative. You can take the appropriate actions to get your act together and improve your situation. Getting a grip is always available, and it's always necessary. It can be hard, but if you want your best life, go for it. You have to get a grip.

To me, getting a grip has a double meaning. Aside from what I just described, it also means a growing recurring income potential. It means taking the initiative and having the drive to be accountable.

I've shown many individuals how to successfully create part-time income and—in many cases—full time careers that have changed their lives. *Get A Grip* focuses on *your* future on this planet. While our longest and most important future will occur after our life on earth, it's important to get a grip while you are here. You can do that through network marketing.

I want you to be happy. I want you to experience whole-someness. I want you to be gung ho. Most of all, I want you to get a grip so that you can change your life. Let's not waste any time. Let's get a grip together.

MAKE *GET A GRIP* WORK FOR YOU

• ◆ •

If you've made it to this page, give yourself a pat on the back. You've committed to getting a grip. You've committed to sitting down, surveying your current situation, examining the pros and cons in your life, and getting your head out of the sand. I'm not saying it's easy, but if you want financial freedom and the opportunity to enjoy your life to the fullest, getting a grip is your first start.

Throughout *Get A Grip*, I'm going to share some incredible experiences the men and women I've worked with in network marketing have had. I'm going to show you just how network marketing has changed thousands of people's lives. It's kept people in their homes, helped them send their children to college, and made them feel absolutely fantastic about themselves and the directions of their lives.

Now, I'm not saying I have all the answers that will solve life's problems, but I have some, and they've come to me via network marketing. I've shown many individuals how to successfully create part-time income and full-time careers through network marketing.

Throughout the next sixteen chapters, I'll show you how to

get a grip through network marketing. At the end of each chapter, I'll give you a few quick, hard-hitting tips so you can go out there today and start getting that grip. At the end of *Get A Grip*, I'll list all sixty-two of these tips so you can get started in network marketing. Now, are you ready to get gung ho about getting a grip?

SECTION 1

••◆••

Get Uplifted

CHAPTER 1
Believe in This Business

• ◆ •

"Network marketing isn't perfect . . .
it's just better."

—Eric Worre

When you're worried about finances, how difficult is it to be creative and productive in other facets of your life? It's impossible. And when you have no prospects, no plans, and no avenues to get yourself past your financial inadequacies, you begin to give up. But you don't have to. There's a light at that end of that tunnel, and that light is called network marketing.

I can't think of another industry that lets you build your own business, be your own boss, and earn part-time income to supplement your existing income the way network marketing does. Now, some people have a bad attitude about network marketing because they don't understand it. They haven't seen it change people's lives, and so they don't believe in it. But success in network marketing is possible—and it's simple. All you have to do is increase product sales through your own efforts plus the efforts of those in your organization until you reach the income you desire. How do you best do that? You:

1. Talk to people regularly and often about your products.
2. Continue to educate customers about the value of your products.
3. Identify those buying your products who will also represent your products and support them strongly.
4. Get referrals from those who recognize the value of your products but who do not wish to personally represent your products.
5. Methodically develop your organization by finding new customers, and leverage your business by finding others to do the same.

We'll get into how you do each of these later. First, I want you to understand what network marketing is really like from someone who has successfully participated in it for decades. So . . . what is network marketing?

It's a Business, Not a Pyramid Scheme

I only started my career in network marketing after I had bought and sold several businesses, and I only went into it because I wanted to. Remember, I didn't need the money, but I was so blown away by how network marketing worked and how it could help people that I got gung ho about it. I'm not the only one.

Network marketing has been endorsed by business leaders and economists all over the world, including *New York Times* best-selling authors David Bach and Robert Kiyosaki. World-renowned economist and forecaster Harry Dent said this about network marketing: "The coming years should be a great time for prospecting in network marketing."

If past years are any measure, Dent is right. In 2016, 107 million people in one hundred countries participated in network marketing, a $182 billion industry globally. In the United States alone, 20.5 million people participated in network marketing in 2016, doing more than $35 billion in retail sales[1].

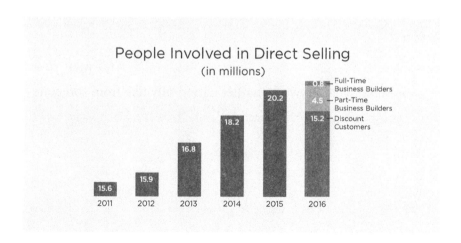

People Involved in Direct Selling
(in millions)

Network marketing is not a pyramid scheme. It's a business, just like every other business. Success depends on how hard you're willing to work at building a customer base. If you can find two customers and create volume through those customers, you've got a business. You get two customers, give them great service, ask for a few referrals, and then watch your volume increase to four, eight, sixteen, and so on.

This model works for thousands of businesses. For example, when I worked for Hanes what did I do? I built customers. How about when I started Robbins Vending? What was I doing then? Building a customer base. Network marketing is like every other business in that it requires building volume and working hard to create that volume, which we'll talk more about in section two.

It's a Life Changer

Network marketing is like other businesses, but it's also a little different because it will change your life in three ways. One, it leverages your efforts better than any other industry can. Two, it immediately improves your quality of life. Three, it puts your earning potential into your hands.

> *Network marketing is like other businesses, but it's also a little different because it will change your life in three ways. One, it leverages your efforts better than any other industry can. Two, it immediately improves your quality of life. Three, it puts your earning potential into your hands.*

How does network marketing do these three things? By creating a recurring income stream for you and your family. Sure, there are plenty of ways to create recurring income. *Buy* a rental property and save enough to buy a second, third, and forth property. *Buy* a franchise and, when it's going well, buy a second, third, and fourth. *Buy* an oil well, and add a second and third. *Buy* a daycare center and increase the number of students over time. *Buy* a car wash, and increase the number of cars being washed by giving great service and creative promotions.

I have personally created recurring income for myself and my family doing every one of those things, but there's one problem with these solutions. They have a tricky word in common: buy. If you already have the financial wherewithal to buy a franchise or rental home, good for you, but most of us simply don't. Even if you can buy one of these opportunities, they still leave you with fixed locations, employees, reports, set hours, and recurring expenses to deal with.

If you start a dry cleaner, for example, you're committing at least $30,000 of your savings and borrowing another $100,000 from a bank. Then there's the lease to think about. Say you commit to a three-year lease of $2,000 a month with utilities at an additional $1,000 a month. Personally, you have to commit to working six days a week, ten hours a day. Say you have a staff of seven people. A year later, after all expenses, you net $1,000 a month.

Now, look at what it costs to start a networking business. It will cost you less than $1,000 to get started (this includes start-up costs and attending local, regional, and/or national trainings during your first year). You don't go in debt, you don't work sixty hours a week, you don't have to pay employees or commit to a fixed location.

If after one year you have enough customers buying your products every month, your income could conservatively be $1,000 a month with you putting in far fewer hours than if you owned a dry cleaner.

I tried the path of building recurring income by owning property and starting businesses with my own capital, but the path I've stuck with is one that isn't encumbered by fixed locations, employees, extensive reporting, or expensive overhead. With network marketing, you can start for next to nothing and keep your current job while you're building your business. You don't have to worry about large expenses or inventory or managing an office.

It's Little Investment with the Greatest Reward

Network marketing requires the least investment and has the best risk/reward ratio of any endeavor I've ever been a part of. That alone will allow you to get a grip.

Imagine asking your boss for a raise next week and being successful. Try to repeat that process the following week. Your boss will think you're crazy! Even crazier, if you ask again the next week. In network marketing, when you increase your volume, you give yourself a raise every week. Every week!

With network marketing, the more you work, the better you're leveraged. I've been in this business for decades, and I've seen hundreds of people leave careers they loved because no matter how hard they worked, they couldn't leverage their own successes. The more you work in this business, the more success you will have. That's not the case in other businesses where you can work as hard as you want and, at the end of the week, you still bring home the same paycheck.

A friend of mine who also works in network marketing was recently asked how much money he had made his first month of network marketing. He answered, "I don't know. I haven't stopped making it."

See, he started with a small number of customers the first month, but some of them were still buying every month. Many years later, he increased his volume and had thousands more people in his organization. That's how networking can grow your recurring income potential. Your efforts today can provide an income for you for years to come. Network marketing leverages your efforts better than any other businesses can.

Just ask my son, Kevin. After college, Kevin went to work for someone in corporate America. He made a good income, but he didn't like getting up early and driving in traffic every morning to work. When he was twenty-seven, I told him about a new network marketing business, but he wasn't interested. He kept doing what he was doing until the stress of his job started getting to him. Not really thinking about where he'd go with network marketing, he started a network marketing business on the side. Kevin made some extra income and paid off some debt working his business part-time for a couple of years. One day, Kevin realized that his side job—network marketing—made almost as much money as his full-time job. He quit his corporate job and he's never looked back. Kevin and his wife, Dawn, have been stay-at-home parents for their two kids. Kevin has traveled with his family to some incredible places and, most importantly, he's been there to watch his kids grow up because he works from home. When you believe in this business, you free yourself to live the life you want to live. Kevin still puts a lot of time into his business, but he works on his time, not on his employer's time.

I love talking to people in my business because every one of them has a story about how network marketing provided a recurring income that improved their quality of life.

From Dairy Farmers to Successful Business Owner

In 1996, I met a woman named Suzanne[2] who lived in Mayfair, which at the time was a thirty-seven-person town in the Canadian province of Saskatchewan. Suzanne lived on a dairy farm that was so remote she had to drive twelve miles to get her mail. You can imagine that a town the size of Mayfair doesn't provide many economic opportunities to its residents. This was a problem for Suzanne. Twenty years earlier, she and her husband had put everything they had into that dairy farm and hadn't taken a vacation since. They were burned out and wanted to get into another business.

A friend told Suzanne about a network marketing opportunity. Despite living in the middle of nowhere, Suzanne drove to the nearest city to hear more. Then she dove right in, flying to the company's convention in Dallas. When she got home, she started talking to people about the company's products. She found many new customers and a few people who also wanted to build a business. In less than two years, Suzanne had earned enough to replace the *entire* income from the dairy farm.

Network marketing gave Suzanne hope, just like it gives millions of other people hope every year. Hope that they can get an answer to their financial problems, which puts them on a path toward getting a grip.

I've said it before and I'll say it again. Money isn't everything. However, it allows you to live a more fulfilling life and, if you're a good person—and I believe you are—you'll become a *better* person when you have a greater capacity to help people.

It is very difficult to grow and develop to your full potential until you've freed yourself from the bonds of financial worry. I've seen many people develop at a much greater pace to their greater benefit when they reach a place free of financial difficulties.

You've got to believe in this business because this business is your path to financial freedom. I came from very little and have reached very high levels of success. I am healthy despite my genetics. I am educated despite my background. I have developed a family that is spirit-filled, joyous, and productive. I have a marvelous, permanent long-time marriage despite having come from a broken family. I am extremely prosperous because of the efforts and ambition that I put forth. I have beaten the odds and you can, too. You just have to believe and apply what you learn.

> *You've got to believe in this business because this*
> *business is your path to financial freedom.*

We can all use network marketing to get a grip. Put your faith in this business, commit to getting a grip, and a year from now, you'll look back and wonder why you didn't do it sooner.

Time to Get a Grip

Eliminate any misconceptions you have about network marketing and understand that it:

1. Is a great industry that lets you build your own business, be your own boss, and control your own income.
2. Has been endorsed by business leaders and economists all over the world.
3. Will change your life by letting you earn more money than other businesses, immediately improving your quality of life and putting your earning potential into your hands.
4. Lets you create recurring income with very little investment.

---

1. http://wfdsa.org/wp-content/uploads/2017/06/Final-Sales-Report-2016-5-26-2017.pdf http://www.dsa.org/docs/default-source/research/growth-outlook/dsa_2016gandofactsheet.pdf?sfvrsn=6

2. All names have been changed.

CHAPTER 2
Believe in Yourself

· ◆ ·

*"Our thinking creates a pathway
to success or failure."*

—Andy Andrews

When I decided to work for Frey Meats in the late 1970s, Donald, the guy who interviewed me, handed me an offer. I looked at it and told him, "If you want me to consider this, you're going to raise your offer substantially."

You see like I said in the introduction, at that point in my career, I'd already had success in numerous businesses and I had the financial freedom to turn down any job I didn't find acceptable. I had the confidence to up Donald's offer. I upped his offer because I *believed in myself.*

No matter which network marketing opportunity you choose, believe in yourself. You need to have the confidence to know you can succeed in this business. If you don't have that belief, you can use the confidence of your sponsor until you develop your own.

If you don't have that confidence right now, or if you feel like you're on a thin ledge, are overworked, under-respected, or underpaid, you're not alone. Many *Get A Grip* readers are in debt with little or nothing in reserves and no prospects for improvement. Maybe your relationships are suffering, your health is bad, or you're being challenged because you feel a sense of inadequacy. If this sounds like you, chances are people know that you're struggling without you saying anything. They know it because you project those hardships to the world. Our lives are tenuous at best and when we feel mean or mousey, we send mean or mousey vibes out to other people. The world sees you the way you see yourself. Make sure your vision of yourself is strong and full of belief.

Program Yourself for Success

The first step in changing this dynamic while also putting yourself in position to get a grip is to program yourself for success. We have been led to believe that we cannot do many things that are actually doable with the right programming, training, and a little practice.

Whether you think you can or you think you can't, you're right! If I didn't think I'd get a better deal from Frey, I wouldn't have. If I didn't think Pac-Man would sell, it wouldn't have. Your programming is self-fulfilling.

We self-prophesize by thinking about how our lives should be, which in turn is what they become. We let our thoughts, our environment, and the people around us program us. Make sure your thoughts lead to success.

Whether you think you can or you think you can't, you're right!

Many people believe that they will always be paid less than what they are worth. That programming severely limits how far they can go. I have always wanted to make more than what I was worth, so I pictured myself making more than I was worth and guess what? It worked. The way I've chosen to program myself has erased every limit anyone has ever put on my potential. You can do the same. Instead of thinking, "I'll never make what I'm worth," tell yourself, "I will make more than I'm worth." It's that simple.

Delight in the Success of Others

When you're learning to reprogram yourself, learn to delight in the successes of others. This is one reason I love network marketing: it makes delighting in the success of others easy.

Network marketing is a selfless business model. Envy does

not fit. Greed or getting ahead of someone else is counterproductive. Why? Because the better someone else does, the better you'll do, too. There is no fairer model. A person brought into the right company today can exceed the accomplishments of those that have been involved for years. One of the greatest attributes of this business is that success only comes to those who extend success to others. It is impossible to build a large, successful organization by yourself. Others in your organization must have success in order for your success to materialize.

This principle doesn't carry through to other industries. In other industries, there's maybe one promotion available a year. Or, if you're in sales, you either close the deal or someone else does. If you try for but do not get that promotion or sale, you do not have the same opportunities for success that you would in an industry that is designed to support others' successes.

Surround Yourself with Positivity

To succeed in anything, surround yourself with positive people and be the positive influence others want to be around.

We are all influenced by the company we keep, the words we say, and the books we read. Make sure those people and those words are the right ones. Make sure they're ones that build you and others up, not ones that bring you down.

Understand that the way you're programmed is reflected in everything you say, do, and accomplish. Build others up, and remember that what you do and say affects the programming of the people who are around you.

It will take time to program yourself correctly, but think about this. If you put a heavy chain around an elephant's leg and drive a spike deep in the ground, the elephant will soon realize it can only go so far, and will eventually stop pulling at the chain and spike. You'll be able to put a less stringent deterrent around the elephant's leg and it still won't pull. Why? Because it's been programmed to think it's restricted. You can do the same thing with your own brain, but in a positive way. That's the beauty of programming.

While you're working on programming yourself for success, try the following:

1. Read a new book or listen to audio.
2. Build your belief about your new company and products from videos, brochures, and online resources or by attending events.
3. Accept your shortcomings.
4. Modify your actions and build upon your successful results.
5. Share these steps with others so they can program themselves for success, too.

Stand on the Shoulders of Giants

One wonderful thing about network marketing is that as your own confidence and abilities develop, you can rely on your sponsor to help build you up. Very few businesses make sure new people have mentors. The mentors in network marketing will help program you for success.

I have personally witnessed thousands who initially lacked belief or confidence become successful in this industry. They learned to rely and depend on the experience and confidence of their mentor or someone in their upline. The incumbent guidance, mentorship, counseling, and confidence available to new people in this business is invaluable.

You only need to bring a willing attitude and a receptive desire to learn, and your ambitions can be fulfilled.

When I was growing up, I was short. I greatly admired the altitude of people who were over six feet tall. I thought being six feet tall and over was the best height until I reprogrammed myself to believe five foot nine was the best height for me. At five foot nine, I can do more than most people can do at six feet. Do the five things I mentioned above, and start reprogramming yourself to be the best that you can be.

As you go through the programming process, try this. When the minute negative thoughts creep into your head or you start feeling like you're projecting something mean or mousey, give yourself an attitude check. As a pilot, when you are flying on instruments, you get the aircraft to the appropriate position by watching a device called an "attitude indicator," which is an artificial aircraft on an artificial horizon. Frequent attitude checks are sometimes necessary. Of course, attitude checks outside of the aircraft are important, too. An accountability partner can help you with your personal attitude checks.

Run through those bad thoughts and reprogram them to work for you. Many of us *think* we can't do things so we don't try. We are what we think. We do what we think we can. Think something great and before you know it, you'll be doing something great, too.

Time to Get a Grip

Program yourself for success today by:

1. Taking a close look at the conversations you have with yourself and how the emotional elements of those conversations project to the world.
2. Give yourself an attitude check. Consider how you approach successes and failures, and commit to approaching both with a positive attitude.
3. Delight in the success of others.
4. Surround yourself with positive people who project what you want from your own life.

CHAPTER 3
Retire with Network Marketing

• ◆ •

"Wealth is the ability to fully experience life."

—Henry David Thoreau

I can't tell you how many people I run into who work hard and do the right thing, but still can't get their heads above water financially. The thing about network marketing is that it can pull you to a position that better prepares you for retirement. Whether you are twenty-five, seventy-five, or somewhere in between, you need to start thinking about your future. Are you going to save your way to your future or, as I demonstrate below, are you going to use network marketing to help you earn your way there?

In August 2014[3], a few years after this country started finding its way out of a devastating recession, *Forbes* contributor and retirement activist Robert Laura wrote a great piece about why network marketing is a great option to help boost retirement savings. First of all, more than half of Baby Boomers are interested in starting their own businesses. Second, even if upcoming retirees don't want to start a business, many of them are realizing they aren't saving enough money to get them through retirement. Third, network marketing offers low barriers to entry making it a fairly easy industry to jump right into. Because network marketing offers flexibility, low barriers to entry, *and* an opportunity to produce recurring income, it's a great way to enhance your retirement savings.

"As a result," Laura wrote, "I believe that the entire industry is poised for explosive growth and can be one of the most significant solutions to America's current retirement savings crisis."

I couldn't agree more. By creating recurring income, network marketing gives thousands of people an opportunity for financial freedom. It allows them to not only pay their bills, but to put money away for retirement that they wouldn't have otherwise had. Just look at my friends Eddie and Tracy.

When Eddie and Tracy got married, they pooled their money so Eddie could buy a truck and go into business for himself. They sacrificed being together so Eddie could spend the hours on the road he needed to get his business going. Before long, Eddie realized his business pretty much owned him. He had no life outside of work. When Eddie and Tracy decided to start a family, Eddie knew things had to change, so he sold the truck to a guy who promised to make monthly payments on the truck. The plan was that the payments would help support the family while Eddie started his new profession as an insurance agent.

Unfortunately, the guy who bought the truck from Eddie never made a single payment. Instead, he filed bankruptcy. Through no fault of his own, Eddie was out a lot of money. Not long after, Eddie and Tracy learned their two kids were suffering from serious and expensive immune system problems. The family maxed out five credit cards trying to live and care for the kids. With no credit left, Eddie and Tracy fell behind on their mortgage payments. To avoid foreclosure proceedings, they gave the bank the $50,000 in equity they'd accrued and moved the family into a trailer.

Follow the Light

Stories like these are heart wrenching. You've got a family that's tried to do everything right—they started their own business, they tried to provide for their children—yet they still fall so desperately behind they simply can't find a way out of their financial challenges. Even when a family took Tracy, Eddie, and the kids in, they still had a mountain of credit card debt and recurring medical bills to pay. They couldn't keep up, let alone think about retirement.

That's when Eddie and Tracey started network marketing. At first, they could hardly pay for the products. Even though startup costs in network marketing are minimal, they were so far down that rabbit hole that it was a struggle to pay for those products. Thankfully, Eddie and Tracy understood that by investing a few hundred dollars, they could create a debt-free future for themselves and their kids. They understood that through network marketing, they could position themselves for retirement by creating recurring income.

Move Toward Financial Freedom

Moving toward financial freedom means creating a source of recurring income that allows you to earn and save money in a way that would be impossible with your average nine-to-five job. An extra $1,000 to $3,000 a month would make a substantial difference to most people. It certainly did for Eddie and Tracy.

> *Moving toward financial freedom means creating a source of recurring income that allows you to earn and save money in a way that would be impossible with your average nine-to-five job.*

Before Eddie and Tracy knew it, they were receiving $3,000 a month through their network marketing business. That $3,000 was enough to supplement Eddie's full-time job as an insurance agent and make a significant difference to his family. Gradually, the couple got out of debt, provided for their family in a way that had been impossible just months before, and started saving for retirement.

Earning an extra $1,000 to $3,000 a month is the first step on the path to financial Freedom, and you can do this with network marketing in a way you can't do it in any other industry. For example, say someone has $1 million in a conservative investment. How much would that money be worth to them monthly? What would their monthly income be? Rates of return vary greatly, as does each person's tolerance for risk, but if this person had the money in a very conservative investment to limit risk, he or she might expect anywhere from $1,000 to $3,000 per month in income.

With network marketing, you can make that $1,000 to $3,000 in a much shorter period of time. What sounds harder? Saving your way to $1 million or working a network marketing business and earning your way to an recurring income source that will allow you to save for retirement? We've seen what it's like to earn your way there. Now let's see what *saving* your way there looks like.

Where Are You Today?

If you look at your current situation and career, how long would it take you to develop a recurring income that would allow you to save $1 million for retirement? Let's take a look:

50 working years remaining = $20,000 savings/year

40 working years remaining = $25,000 savings/year

30 working years remaining = $33,333 savings/year

20 working years remaining = $50,000 savings/year

10 working years remaining = $100,000 savings/year

For most people, this simple calculation is eye opening and not always in a good way. Even if you invest your money in the hopes of growing it faster, you may only grow at a conservative 3 to 5 percent annually with a risk of losing some principle along the way in a volatile market. Even with investments, if you've got numerous working years left—say fifty—are you in a position where you can save $20,000 a year? Most people would say no, which is why I want to show you how to create a recurring income that will do this for you.

In network marketing, many people focus on the huge incomes of the top distributors. Certainly, those incomes are attainable by some, and I have personally helped many people reach six-figure incomes. However, I believe success can be found in network marketing at much lower levels and in much shorter time frames. Start with a goal of earning just a few hundred dollars/month. Remember, you only need to find a few customers and then create leverage by finding distributors who will also have customers and other distributors. As that volume grows, so will your potential. Once you prove to yourself that you can earn a few hundred dollars, you'll have the confidence to grow your business into the $1,000 to $3,000 range.

Where Do You Want to Be Tomorrow?

Think about how $1,000 to $3,000 of extra monthly income would affect your life. Think about how it would affect the next six months, year, two years, or five years of your life. There's a big difference, right?

If you're like me, personal budgets simply never work. Something always comes up. There's always an unexpected expense that derails whatever good intention I had with my budget. Expect that things will always happen and prepare for them by setting yourself up to create this recurring income source.

Creating recurring income through network marketing lets you get ahead and build reserves. If you constantly feel like you're struggling because you're overcommitted financially, aren't disciplined with your spending, or are always running into unexpected expenses, don't downsize, postpone, or reduce your budget. Develop a plan to *make more money than you spend.*

Stop watching TV or playing around on social media. Stop wasting hour after hour of your life and commit to developing a plan to create recurring income. Start working a network marketing business during your non-productive television time.

Use Your Hours Wisely

How many hours are there in the week? I love asking people this question. They always respond with some variation of "um," and then trail off to think about it. There are 168 hours in every week. I know this because to me, each one of those hours is precious and I want to make sure that I spend each one of those 168 hours doing what I want to do.

I rarely wake to an alarm clock. I stay in bed until I'm finished sleeping whenever that might be, and when I wake up, I spend time with my family. If I didn't have this recurring income—if I didn't have money working for me every single month—I couldn't do this. I'd be up with an alarm, spending my time commuting to an office so I could make money for someone else on his or her time.

Most people spend their life worrying about money. When you get to a point where you're not thinking about money all the time, you will be better off. You will be happier, healthier, and more capable of helping those around you. Money causes so many unnecessary problems in people's relationships. It causes numerous marital conflicts that often lead to divorce. You don't have to live like that. You don't have to hope and pray that nothing happens this month so you can save $100 by the end of it. How much you make and how early you set yourself up for retirement is one hundred percent up to you.

Time to Get a Grip

Want to retire through network marketing?
Ask yourself the following:

1. At my current salary level and savings rate, how long will it take for me to save enough money to retire?

2. How would generating $1,000 to $3,000 a month help myself and my family? What stress would it relieve?

3. What activities can I reduce or stop altogether (watching TV, social media) that would free up more time for me to pursue this idea of creating recurring income for myself?

4. How can I develop a plan today to make more money than I spend?

3. http://www.forbes.com/sites/robertlaura/2014/08/29/would-you-join-a-multi-level-marketing-company-for-retirement-income/#10bca60f769a

SECTION 2

·◆·

Get Started

CHAPTER 4
Get Started

• ◆ •

"One business model stands out . . .
creates passive income . . .
little cash investment . . .
low overhead . . . part time basis . . .
generates enough . . . to transition out of . . .
full time income job . . . network marketing."

—Robert Kiyosaki

There are many unique things about network marketing and the opportunities it provides millions of people, but the one thing that network marketing has in common with every business is that it's a business. And, just like if you started a laundromat, car wash, or restaurant, your approach to network marketing has to be methodical and consistent and you *must* show up.

Like we talked about in chapter one, the main thing you need to do to succeed in network marketing is increase your sales volume. The only methodical way to do this is to treat your network marketing opportunity as a business even if you only have five to ten hours a week to do it.

Get Serious

One of the best things about network marketing is that you can do it on the side while you're working full-time for someone else. I love this because it has allowed many people, who wouldn't otherwise have had the time, to develop recurring income. The one down side to doing something on the side that costs so little to start is that there's a risk that you might not take it seriously.

Years ago, this nice Texas couple, George and Carol, started looking for career changes. George worked in trust operations for what was then Nations Bank. Carol traveled internationally for a technology company. They were busy and had good, well-paying jobs, but they were exhausted. When George told Carol he no longer liked his job, they started looking for another way.

Every business opportunity George and Carol looked into cost at least $100,000 to get started. Although they could have cashed out their retirement funds and maybe made one of these opportunities work, it was too much of risk. That's when George and Carol came across a network-marketing seminar. They started asking questions, and before they knew it, they found themselves trying the product. Not long after, they got serious about their network marketing opportunity.

The first few months following George and Carol's decision to go into network-marketing were hectic. They both continued working full-time and didn't have more than a few hours a week to market the product. However, they did one thing right, they focused on the few hours they did have for their new opportunity seriously.

Now, if your goal is to create recurring income for yourself and your family and you want to do that by working just a few hours a week, good for you, but commit to those few hours and give them everything you've got. That's what George and Carol did when they started. Before they knew it, their business developed a mind of its own. One month, they had sixty contacts. The following month, they had 120. By the third month, they had more than 200! Seven months after George and Carol started their network marketing business, George left the bank. Not long after, Carol followed George's lead and left her job, too. They continued working hard on their business, but instead of working for someone else, they worked for themselves.

I want to point out that quick success, like the success that George and Carol had, doesn't occur frequently. Of course, it never occurs for those who don't make an effort. Even if it takes numerous years to reach that level of success, it's worth it.

Get Committed

This business will develop a mind of its own if you let it, but you must be committed.

As I said before, even if your goal is to build your business five-to-ten hours every week, then commit to those hours. According to the Nielson media ratings company[4], the average American watches more than five hours of TV every day. Every day! If you think you don't have time to commit five hours a week to this business, cut your TV watching by one hour every day and you'll have five hours a week to focus on your business.

Get Invested

I doubt that any other entrepreneurial industry has given as many people a true shot at financial independence as network marketing has, especially with so little initial investment. Carol and George only spent $1,000 in their network marketing business during their first year. That $1,000 even includes some travel expenses to get proper training at a conference. Many people can get started for much less.

I always tell people there isn't a business in America that has the potential to make money more with such a minimal investment.

I'm investing in a series of restaurants right now. That's a $700,000 investment for a 1,000-square-foot space. That's expensive. If those restaurants don't do well, I'm out a lot of money. It's much easier to get started in a network marketing business, and it has very little risk. If you don't put the necessary time in to work it, at least you haven't lost a huge investment. So don't be afraid to go for it!

To get started in this business, you need to get a grip, stop doing things that aren't worthwhile, and *commit* to developing your own financial security. Expect to develop your business and reap great rewards. Give it ALL you have. It will be worth it.

Time to Get a Grip

To get started in network marketing, understand that:

1. The minimal sacrifices you make today have the potential to drastically change your life ten years from now.

2. No other business model allows its owners to start with such a small investment.

3. Even if you only want to work in network marketing five to ten hours a week, you must commit to those five to ten hours.

4. Like every other business out there, your approach to network marketing must be methodical.

---

4. http://www.nydailynews.com/life-style/average-american-watches-5-hours-tv-day-article-1.1711954

5. It should be noted that regulators no longer allow for large start up fees however, it is appropriate to pay for travel and training.

CHAPTER 5

Pick a Company

• ◆ •

*"Network marketing is a
low-investment, low-overhead
business in which common people
can achieve amazing results."*

—Presley Swagerty

Once you decide this business is for you, you need to choose a
company. There are hundreds of networking opportunities out
there, but not all opportunities are created equally. You want to
make sure the company you choose is sustainable, has a good
compensation plan, and sells proprietary products that you can
get excited about.

Choose Sustainability

Of all the network marketing companies out there, you want to choose one that has demonstrated success. Choosing a company that hasn't demonstrated success puts you at risk of spending a great deal of effort investing time, energy, and money into something that won't put you on the path toward financial freedom.

When you start looking at network marketing companies, choose one that has been developed for the long run. Don't fall for those enticing ground floor opportunities or flashy new startups. It may be tempting—the product may look good, the company might have a lot of snazzy materials—but be careful. Usually if you hear someone say, "If you are one of the first ones in, you'll have the best chance at making the most money," it's time to turn and run. Why? Because this is false logic.

A legitimate network marketing opportunity is based on your own production of selling product and empowering other leaders to do the same. The opportunity should be the same for someone on day one as it is for someone who has been with the company for twenty years. If you hear a phrase like, "Get in first while the opportunity is hot," the business is likely being built on hype and will not be a long-lasting vehicle for you.

The company you choose doesn't have to be a $1 billion company, but it does need to have a track record of success. The reality is that many new companies are formed every month. According to *Forbes*[6], "Ninety percent of startups will fail." Most of those will fail within the first three years. Thus, I recommend that you find a company that is *at least three years* old that has demonstrated some staying power.

Any time I've invested in a business or a product, I've done my research. I've looked at the people running the company, the company's reputation, its financials, its product, and its future forecasts. Do this when you're trying to decide which network company to choose.

Just because a company is seemingly growing fast doesn't mean it's going to last. Many times a fast-growing company doesn't have the capital to grow quickly. It won't be able to meet the needs of its customers or distributors. Soon, it may have lengthy backorders, shipping delays—or even worse—it may start delaying checks. A financially strong company can survive in growth or in times of retraction. The best companies will go up, down, and then up again. A weak company will go out of business if the business grows or contracts too quickly.

Read the company's mission statement carefully. It will tell you a lot about the heart, direction, and integrity of the company, as well as who is attracted to it. Evaluate the benevolence of the company. Do they want to accomplish more than just bottom line profit? Looking at each of the components mentioned here will help you choose a solvent network marketing opportunity that is right for you.

Choose Experience and Culture

When you're looking at companies, don't just look at how long they've been in business or their financials. Many times, you'll see that the CEO or the executives stay for a year and then move to another company. You want to make sure these key people are committed to the company and aren't likely to run off whenever a new opportunity comes around.

Check out the credentials of key management, paying particularly close attention to their experience in network marketing. Talented, experienced management with successful track records understand how to support the people they work with and appreciate the field sales activities much better than those who do not have a history with network marketing.

To get the feel for the company and how you might like working with it, attend company events and feel the spirit of the people who participate in it. Do they welcome you? Do you feel at home around them? Is there an attitude of diversity and acceptance? Do you witness frequent, cordial greetings between both old and new acquaintances? Is there an air of enthusiasm and excitement that is not hype? Would you want your closest friends and relatives to witness these gatherings and visit with the people that are working this endeavor? This last question is important. The more you like a company, the more you feel supported by it and have faith in its direction and management, the harder you'll want to work for it.

The more you like a company, the more you feel supported by it and have faith in its direction and management, the harder you'll want to work for it.

If top leaders exhibit a high level of elitism, almost to the point of worship, I recommend walking away. This kind of attitude toward others is not healthy. Healthy recognition for accomplishments is important. However, I believe new leaders should be honored and respected as much as those who have been around a long time. A continual flow of new customers and leaders is the greatest asset in any business.

Choose a Seamless Compensation Plan

Another thing to look for is the company's commission structure. You want one that's seamless so that no matter where new customers come from, your opportunity to grow your business will remain the same.

Compensation in this industry works a little bit differently than it does in other industries, but it also gives the people within it a greater opportunity to make more money. In a traditional sales position—say the position involves selling shoes—a salesperson may earn a 30 percent commission on every sale. So, for every pair of shoes sold, he or she gets a 30 percent commission. In network marketing, instead of paying the entire commission to one person, that same commission is stretched over multiple levels, which allows you to earn commissions on many more customers.

For example, instead of paying one person a 30 percent commission, that commission could be stretched out to 10 percent over three levels. This creates an opportunity for leverage. Instead of being paid on your own efforts and your efforts alone, you can be paid based on the efforts of many others. You're not only paid for your own customer volume, you're also paid for the customer volume generated by others on your team. This leverage is what creates an incentive for you to want to help many others attain success. Their success is your success.

As industrialist John Paul Getty, who was named the Richest Living Man in America in 1957 by *Forbes* magazine, once said, "I'd rather earn one percent off 100 people's efforts, than 100 percent off my own efforts." Network marketing lets you do this.

Most products that are sold by a retail distribution model, such as clothes, coffee, or makeup, factor in many layers of middlemen and advertising costs. Often, advertising these products represents 40 to 50 percent of the cost of the product. So, when you spend $4 on a sugary latte, roughly $2 of that goes toward advertising. That's just the way business works. Network marketing companies spend very little or nothing at all on advertising. Instead of paying actors or athletes to entice customers to buy products, network marketing companies pay regular people like you and me to create word-of-mouth advertising. If you like a product, you tell other people about it. With the *right* business model, you can actually get paid for that.

Product Value = More Customers = More Money

Just like there are overpriced products in every industry, there are some overpriced products in the network marketing industry. Before you choose a company, make sure that the products or services from your chosen company are competitive in the marketplace. Ask yourself:

1. Are they unique?
2. Do they have value?
3. Will people purchase them who are not distributors?

This goes back to the equation I mentioned at the beginning of the book:

Product value = more customers = more money

When you have a product or service that can change someone's quality of life or solve a problem for them, then you can find new customers for that product. Any network marketing opportunity that you choose must be based on this principle. Start with a goal of finding just two customers. Give them great service, and ask them if there is anyone else they know who would appreciate using the product. Many companies will offer discounts on their product orders by giving referrals. If you find two customers, you'll see how easily it is to turn that into four customers, six customers, eight customers, and so on. When those customers like the product, they will buy again generating more monthly product volume.

Some of the people that you talk to will be interested in making some extra income just like you, so they'll do the same thing you did. They'll put customers first. Eventually, by using this leverage, you can create a team of hundreds or even thousands of customers to buy your product each month.

Choose Proprietary Products

A proprietary, patented, or patent pending technology means that other companies will not readily copy you. This provides a strong competitive edge. You don't want to educate a lot of people about the value of something only to find it on retail shelves everywhere you go.

I've made the mistake of not working with propriety products. Guess what happened? Soon those products were in retail stores. You don't want to invest your time and energy into a product only to realize two months later that it's in every retail store in America.

Choose Products that Excite You

When you're looking at products, ask yourself, "Is this product or service something I'm interested in?"

In other words, can you get excited about the product? Don't let someone tell you that the product doesn't matter, that this business is only about the *opportunity*. Take it from someone who has spent more than thirty years in the industry, the product *always* matters. I wouldn't have sold a single product for any of the many businesses I owned if I didn't believe in the product. Do not pick a product that doesn't excite you!

It's much easier to talk to someone about a product or service when you have a passionate interest in it. You've got to remember that your job is to get other people interested in the product. If you don't have interest in the product, there's no way anyone you talk to will either. Enthusiasm is valuable. It literally means, "God within and overflowing."

Companies that tell you the product doesn't matter usually have substandard, overpriced products. If customers won't buy the product on its own merit, eventually the company will fail. When you're looking at companies, ask what percentage of people only buy the products as customers. The answer will speak volumes about the product's value. If a high percentage of the product's users are only customers, that gives you a good indication to value of the product.

Take your time choosing your company and your product because that choice will dramatically affect your results. I know a couple—Dave and Karen—who interviewed many companies before choosing their networking opportunity. They looked at everything from compensation to product to the people behind the curtain. The incredible thing is, before interviewing these companies, Karen had been in network marketing for years! She knew what she was doing, and she still took the time to find the right company. Because Dave and Karen did their homework, because they found a sustainable company they could get gung ho about, they had phenomenal success.

While you don't have to interview every company, do your research. Your success depends on your product, the company, and how hard you work. Pick a company that honors the product, the business opportunity, and the purpose.

Time to Get a Grip

When you start looking at product, consider the following:

1. Is the company selling a sustainable product?
2. Does the company have a seamless compensation plan?
3. Is the product proprietary?
4. Is the product something I can personally get excited about?
5. What percentage of people who buy the product buy it as customers only?

---

6. http://www.forbes.com/forbes/welcome/?toURL=http://www.forbes.com/sites/neilpatel/2015/01/16/90-of-startups-will-fail-heres-what-you-need-to-know-about-the-10/&refURL=https://www.google.com/&referrer=https://www.google.com/

CHAPTER 6
Develop Your Plan

• ◆ •

"Always plan ahead. It wasn't raining when Noah built the ark."

—Richard Cushing

How much time do you spend thinking about *why* you do the job you do? If you're like most people, the answer is, "Not much." Maybe in the beginning you chose your career because you thought it would be rewarding or you thought you could make good money doing it. However, as time has passed, things have changed.

Today, some people have jobs they love and have purpose in. Sadly though, many people get out of bed every morning and go to work for one reason: to not get fired. That may not be something they think about consciously, but they know deep down that if they stay at home and don't go to work, they probably won't have a job tomorrow. For those people, not getting fired is their *why*. Not getting fired is their prime incentive for going through each day. I'm not saying these people do a poor job at work. They may do GREAT work; however, the majority of people don't have to think about why they do what they do each day.

One of the major advantages to network marketing is that you don't have a boss. Your why can be so much bigger and more impactful than, "I don't want to get fired." Network marketing allows you to find a purpose in your work that becomes your reason—your why—for getting up and putting in the hours every day.

> *One of the major advantages to network marketing is that you don't have a boss.*

This wonderful advantage is a blessing, but it also can be a curse. What happens when no one forces you to get out and talk to people? What happens when no one stands over your shoulder forcing you to make calls?

Without being highly motivated, it's often too easy to quit at the first sign of negativity. It's easy to say, "forget about it," when a potential customer tells you no. This is why you have to develop your purpose—your reason—for going into network marketing.

Know Your Why

The only way to overcome no is to have a rock solid why or reason for being in this business, and it can't have anything to do with how much money you want to make. Specifically, you need to ask yourself, "Why am I going to stick with this business when someone tells me no?"

There are numerous reasons for staying persistent with this business. Your *why* may be that you want to be free of a nine-to-five job, or that you want to save enough money to take your family on that vacation that you've always wanted to take, or that you want to end those fights with your spouse about money so you can start having a better relationship, or that you want to visit one of your kids who moved across the country several years ago. Whatever your reason—whatever your why—get it in your head and return to it whenever you hear "no" because no matter what business you get into, "no" is part of the business.

If you develop and return to a why that exists outside of financial goals, that why will supersede any anxieties you have over picking up the phone to make a call or send a text. It will give you courage when someone reacts negatively to your new business. It will eliminate your desire to sit on the couch and watch TV in the evening. If your why is specific enough, if you know your exact purpose for starting in network marketing, then you will have the motivation to do the activities necessary to accomplish your goals.

I know a couple, Marc and Ann, who have always lived a purpose filled-life. In 1990, they started a church in the south Seattle area and spent years working with families. In 1993, Ann started experiencing health problems, which of course affected the whole family.

Marc came across some products that almost immediately helped Ann feel better. These products introduced Marc to a network marketing opportunity. In 1999, the couple decided to leave their church in the care of another family. They found their new purpose was to help other people improve their health and improve their financial situation by sharing these products, which were available through network marketing. Marc and Ann's strong desire to help others was their *why* and that why sustained them when they experienced nos or had other doubts about their new career.

No matter which products or company you choose, you must find a purpose that's greater than financial gain.

Set Your Goals

If you keep doing what you are doing now, where will you be in ten years? How about in twenty years? Would you like to change that future?

Network marketing is a long-term solution that can change your life. When you start in network marketing, you need to look at your long-term goals and decide where you want to be in the next year, five years, and ten years. From there, you can build short-term goals that will help you reach those long-term outcomes.

If your short-term goal is to work at network marketing five hours a week, then work at it five hours a week. If it's to leave your full-time job in two years, set daily goals that will allow you to reach that two-year goal. Your goals should always return to your why because that's the thing that will sustain you when you've had a rough day or someone puts doubt in your mind about your own abilities. I personally like to modify my goals periodically, so write them in pencil intentionally. I make my goals in small, attainable steps so that I can accomplish them!

Commit to Your Actions

Each of your short-term goals should be action oriented. If you want to make enough money to pay off your debt and take your family on a vacation, you must write down which *actions* you need to take *each day* to hit that goal. Maybe your short-term goal is to call two new people every day before noon. That's a great goal because it's an activity. You either do it or you don't. You can't set goals for yourself without any action behind them because then you're not doing.

I always tell people to write their goals in pencil. If you write them in pencil, they're realistic because you can modify them. If your goal is to call two new people every day, but you try to meet that goal for a week and realize you are getting better results by sending text messages instead, then modify your goal. You'll still reach your long-term goal, but instead of feeling bad about yourself for not making those calls, you'll feel good about contacting new people.

You do not want to set yourself up for failure or negative thinking. If your active goal isn't working, modify it so you are successful every day. Who knows? In a few months, you might find yourself raising your goals. You might see yourself *improve* and then your new goal can reflect that improvement.

I always advise people to share their activity-related goals with someone on their team. I find that when you verbalize those goals, you have a much better chance of making them happen. It makes you accountable. Think about it. If you're trying to lose weight, are you more likely to stick to those goals if you go to the gym by yourself every day or if you commit to going with a group of friends?

Whatever your goals, the only way to get a grip and make them a reality is to make sure they're action-oriented, realistic, and accountable.

Time to Get a Grip

Network marketing is great because it allows you to determine your life's purpose. Do that by:

1. Asking yourself, "Why am I going to stick with this business when someone tells me no?"
2. Developing a long-term goal that has nothing to do with financial outcomes.
3. Looking at your long-term goals and deciding where you want to be in the next year, five years, and ten years.
4. Building short-term goals that include specific actions that will help you reach those long-term outcomes.
5. Writing your goals in pencil and then sharing them with your team.

CHAPTER 7
Use Your Tools

• ♦ •

"Our success should not be a random event, but the result of conscious actions."

—Tony Jeary

If something makes your job easier, makes you more efficient, or gives you better results, it's a tool.

Like most industries, network marketing is full of tools. No matter which network marketing opportunity you choose, you'll have access to books, magazines, videos, online planning aids, social media, brochures, pamphlets, audios, videos, and testimonials from customers who love the product.

These tools will help you become more effective at what you do. Tools will help you make a presentation and help you follow up with a new prospect. They can add validation, and they can even help you close. Tools can do a lot of the work for you so you can focus on building a relationship and building trust in your product or company. Tools keep things simple.

How to Choose the Right Tools

Every job has tools that are necessary to the day-to-day function of that job. Imagine a surgeon without a scalpel, a carpenter without a hammer, or an infantryman without a weapon. Without those tools, none of these professionals could complete the basic requirements of their jobs. Just like professionals in every other industry, network marketing requires that you find the tools necessary for your business.

Because there are so many tools out there, the tools you choose—the tools that will work wonderfully for you—will not be the same tools that work well for me. Every person who goes into network marketing needs to test different tools to see which work the best.

When I talk to people about this business, I use one tool that's worked for me for decades. My tool is retirement. Whenever I show people what their retirement looks like based on what they're doing today and contrast that with how their retirement will look after they start earning extra income with network marketing, I capture their interest. For me, this tool is fantastic.

With this tool, I help people see how many customers they need to work with to reach their retirement goals. So, if they want to make $1,000 a month through network marketing, I show them how they need to increase their volume year over year to reach that goal. For me, this tool is highly effective; however, it doesn't work for everyone.

My son, Kevin, whose story about giving up a lucrative corporate career for network marketing I shared in chapter one, never talks to people about how network marketing will affect their retirement goals. Instead, Kevin uses PowerPoint presentations and company videos that are effective for his audience. We both have different approaches and we've both found tools—different from each other's—to support those approaches.

Some of my other favorite tools include:

www.success.com

www.networkingtimes.com

The Little Black Book of Scripts by Todd Falcone

Think and Grow Rich by Napoleon Hill

Rich Dad, Poor Dad by Robert Kiyosaki

Brilliant Compensation by Tim Sales (video)

Go Pro by Eric Worre

Books, including *Get A Grip*, are a great field resource. Highlight and underline key passages and know where you can send others to corroborate points you are teaching. While you're in the field, you also might want to watch short YouTube videos that demonstrate your product, and have them readily available.

While *reading* advice passed down from experts is certainly valuable, listening to the experts and talking to them *face to face* is also a great way to build your business. One of the biggest shortcomings in networking marketing is that people don't spend enough time with each other. Going to the destination meetings put on by your company and meeting people face to face is incredibly valuable. In fact, this one-on-one contact is one of the greatest ways to learn about success from successful people. Meet people face to face *whenever you get the chance.* Not only does this mean going to company destination meetings, it also means grabbing every opportunity you have to meet with friends, customers, and other people whose relationships you find valuable.

One of my other favorite tools is three-way calling. This allows someone else to be the expert when they are speaking to your new potential customer or business associate. If you are speaking to one of your contacts (a friend, neighbor, or family member) they know you for what you do. You may be a teacher or an accountant or a stay-at-home mom. They may not look to you as an expert in starting a business. However, if you add someone else (a business owner) to the call whom your friend, neighbor, or family member doesn't know, your contact will initially listen to that person with more interest and respect.

It's important to introduce both people on the call. Let's say John is your friend and Sarah is your new business partner. You might say, "John, I invited Sarah on the phone because she's been working with the company I told you about for a couple of years. Sarah just got back from taking her family on a great incentive trip with the company. I thought she could better explain the product and company to you."

Then say, "Sarah, I wanted to introduce you to my friend

John. We go to church together. John's one of the sharpest people I know, and he's the first person I thought of who might be interested in hearing about this opportunity."

Keep the conversation light and fun and don't be too serious. After the introductions, be quiet and let Sarah take over.

I hope you can see why I love three-way calling. Use it regularly, and then show other people on your team how to do it.

Avoid Overload

Have you ever been doing many things on your computer at once and bam, that multicolored wheel starts spinning? Everything stops working. That little wheel is your computer's way of saying, "You're giving me too much. Information overload." The same principle applies to your network marketing tools.

I've seen far too many people start this business by trying out every single tool available to them. They go to every conference, watch every video, and read every book. When this happens, they focus more on going to conferences and building their tool library than they do getting appointments, meeting people, and selling their product. Of course, when this happens, they don't have any time to get customers—and you can't run a business without customers.

While it's important to find tools that work for you, you also need to focus on the main thing. In this business, the main thing is doing the activities that directly increase your volume.

Don't Be Afraid of Change

When you're deciding which tools to use, remember that the tools you use today might not be the tools you use tomorrow. Five years from now, you may find a tool that works for you today is no longer working. That's okay. Try another tool.

Technology will dramatically impact the tools available to you. When I first started in network marketing, we didn't have cell phones, the Internet, or social media. Today, cell phones, the Internet, and social media are some of our best tools. If the people in this business were closed to those innovations, they would miss out on huge networking opportunities. Your tools and the way they are delivered will change. Be open to those changes.

Always stay on top of your tools. Sometimes, the tools you used to use will be flat out wrong. Old brochures and marketing materials can have the wrong prices or an incomplete list of current products. Make sure your marketing tools are always up to date, and occasionally look at your other tools to see if they're still relevant.

Time to Get a Grip

Effectively use your tools by:

1. Finding the tools that work the best for you.
2. Ensuring that you don't get so wrapped up in exploring various tools that you stop doing the main thing, which is building volume.
3. Being open to trying out new tools, especially as they experience technological changes.

CHAPTER 8
Never Quit

• ◆ •

*"An ounce of action is worth
a ton of theory."*

—Ralph Waldo Emerson

One of the biggest myths about network marketing is that you just sign up, talk to one or two people, and the money starts rolling in. It doesn't happen that way. If those are your expectations, or if you have spoken with someone who implied this business is that simple, you will fail. To be successful in this industry, you must work, and you can never quit. You must put the time in.

When many people talk about network marketing, they talk about it as the "deferred gratification" business. Why? Because to do well, you need patience. It takes time to create the leverage necessary to be successful. Success is not immediate.

Let's look at the work/income ratio in this business.

After a few months of work, work, work, work, work, and little money, you may get discouraged. Your brother-in-law may say, "See, I told you so. Network marketing is too good to be true."

You have to be patient and remember that you are an entrepreneur. There isn't a single successful businessman or businesswoman who made a fortune the day they opened their business. Every one had to practice patience and work hard to earn their success.

> *You have to be patient and remember that you are an entrepreneur. There isn't a single successful businessman or businesswoman who made a fortune the day they opened their business.*

If you don't understand that it takes work and time to be successful, then you will doubt yourself. You will start to believe your brother-in-law, and soon you will quit. If you quit working, then I promise you won't succeed.

WORK............................MONEY

WORK...MONEY

WORK.........................**MONEY**

Sometimes we quit because failure can feel uncomfortable. Whenever I think about this topic, I remember the family ski vacation we took years ago, when my kids were still living at home. At the end of the day, my wife said, "What a great day. I didn't fall once." She was happy about this, but my sons had a different take. They explained that if they didn't fall several times a day, it would be their worst day of skiing ever. Why? Because to them, a day without falling meant a day without learning or trying new things. You must fall, or fail, to learn.

I love this story because it applies directly to business. You need to be prepared to work and learn from the mistakes you make along the way to be successful.

Take Joy in What You Do

The reason people come up short in most endeavors is that they either don't work enough or they don't work smart enough. Lack of work means your *why*, which we talked about in chapter six, is not in place. It means you haven't determined why you're doing what you're doing, which makes it difficult to get motivated.

You need to get to a place where you enjoy what you do. With the right attitude, work is much easier. This leads to more success because nothing creates success better than success itself.

Work with Intensity

If you want to catapult your networking business, start with intensity. Earlier, I said that you can do this business by putting in only five to ten hours per week, a schedule that will require some patience. To start your business with intensity means putting as many hours as possible into your business at the beginning. That might mean spending forty hours a week working your full-time job and then many more hours a week in your network marketing business, but that intensity will pay off in the long run.

Most people who fail in this business fail because they expect full-time results quickly while only working in network marketing a small amount each week. If you want faster results, start with intensity.

Think about how a pilot gets an airplane off the ground. They don't ease into takeoff. They hit full throttle. That's intensity. In the beginning, they give it everything they've got. It isn't until they reach a certain level that they relax a little. They ease off because they hit cruising altitude.

In this industry, cruising altitude is reaching a full-time income. This is when you can stop working for someone else and start working full-time for yourself.

Work the Basics

After you develop your *why* and commit to using your time wisely, your daily/weekly activities should include:

1. Adding to your list of people who may be interested in your product or business.
2. Using scripts for contacting your list.
3. Inviting people to learn about your product or business.
4. Doing three-way calls with your sponsor.
5. Attending meetings and bringing new people to those meetings.
6. Developing yourself.
7. Committing to and expecting accountability.
8. Talking and listening to clients, the people you work with, and the people you want to learn from.

For many people, network marketing starts as a part-time business. If this is the case for you, you might not have time to go full throttle at first. If that's the case, be productive with the time you do have. Schedule your hours and dedicate 20 to 25 percent of your time to educating yourself and investing in personal development. The rest of your time should be focused on the main thing, which is making new contacts and talking to those contacts about your product or business.

Take Action

Working hard means taking action. A number of activities lead to success in network marketing. While many people are more than willing to be active, they over emphasize certain activities to keep busy and under emphasize activities that count the most.

I'm not opposed to any activities that will help you succeed; however, I've seen far too many people limit their own success by putting too much energy into lower-value activities when they should put their energy into higher-value activities.

If you let them, some activities can become diversions from what counts the most. The main thing is always the main thing: talk to people about your products and opportunities.

Look at this chart to see which activities you should be most focused on today.

Activity	Points/Weighting
Read a book	5
Study your product	5
Watch a video	5
Add a new contact	5
Attend a local meeting	10
Make a call/send text to prospect	10
Make a follow up call/text	10
Attend a training	20
Make an appointment	20
Make a presentation	30
Make a presentation with your upline	40
Sponser a new customer	80
Sponser a new distributor	80
Help someone on your team rank-up	100

If you focus on the higher-level activities, you will maximize the time you have to start your new business.

No Excuses

If you work hard in this business and commit to never giving up, you will succeed. People from all walks of life have done just that. Take a look at one such wonderful person who I worked with.

Janet was a nurse. She was a smart, thoughtful, analytical lady. She was wise beyond belief and wasn't given to risk taking or exaggeration. In fact, she was so committed to thinking *through* things, that she often attended silent retreats.

When Janet first got into network marketing, she was worried her reserved personality wouldn't work with the business. Thankfully, someone had the foresight to tell Janet that if she focused on the right activities, the fact that she wasn't a high-energy person wouldn't matter. Within ten days of receiving her product, Janet signed up ten people. After seven months, Janet was making more than she ever expected! Janet took the advice she was given, focused on high-value activities, persevered, and put herself in a great position to create recurring income for retirement.

The Nike slogan "Just Do It" is one of my favorites. I'm all for study and preparation, but ultimately you must decide to take a leap to make something happen. Force the issue!

Time to Get a Grip

Anyone who has started a business knows that at some point, you feel like giving up. The successful ones don't. When you feel like quitting:

1. Know that to succeed in every industry, you must persist.
2. Be patient. There isn't a single successful businessman or businesswoman who made a fortune the day they opened their business.
3. Focus on the activities and actions that have the greatest potential to grow your business.
4. Commit to never giving up and you will succeed.

CHAPTER 9
Find Your Aces

• ♦ •

"Leaders must absolutely be self-starters. Personal initiative is not optional for a leader."

—Chris Brady/Orrin Woodward

As we've discussed, it takes time to build volume in this business. But if you work hard, have a strong *why,* and focus on the right activities, you will eventually build that volume. Once you do, you'll want to focus on building at least four legs of your business.

I know there are many different compensation plans in network marketing, but regardless of your specific plan, developing at least four legs over time is usually a strong strategy.

Each leg has one distributor at the top who you directly sponsored. Then, the leg contains all the customers and other distributors that flow from that one distributor.

Among the distributors will be many part timers who also have customers and other distributors. However, in each of these legs, you will be looking to develop a leader, or what I call an ace, that will help create and sustain recurring income for you. Together, the leader from each leg will make up your four aces.

Who Are the Four Aces?

A deck of cards has fifty-two cards and among those fifty-two cards are four aces. In network marketing, it is important to find the aces who will help you drive your business to a much higher place. Aces are dynamic, personable, highly respected, and capable of making things happen very quickly. They tend to reach higher incomes and will drive and motivate others on your team.

In this industry, success comes from finding the right partners to work with. These people—your aces—are ambitious, hard-working, and giving . . . and you only need four of them to take your business to the next level.

Your four aces must be in different legs of your business. Think of them like the aces in a deck of cards. Spades work with spades, hearts work with hearts, and so on. Each ace will have discernible differences like a heart, club, spade, and diamond. Some aces may be sponsored by you, but more than likely, your aces will be sponsored by someone else.

I have aces many levels down in my organization. My aces are the reason that I've had and continue to have so much success in network marketing. Get your business started, work hard, and start looking for those aces.

What Does an Ace Look Like?

An ace is usually outgoing and involved. They volunteer in the community, constantly talk to people, and consistently grow their businesses. They are willing learners, they show up at all meetings and all events, they love life, and they are busy.

Aces are also dreamers. They think life should be grand. They do not want to be normal because they are unwilling to accept the rut that is "being normal." They are ambitious, but not in a greedy sense. They reach out to others. They enjoy having fun, but they also enjoy working. They delight in success, both their own and that of others. They love to be part of other's successes.

Aces also appreciate recognition. They seek it, but they also readily recognize others. They love to lift people up. They are natural encouragers whom people want to be around. They have attractive, productive personalities.

Most Aces love the word *legacy*—and they love the meaning of *legacy*. They want to change the world for the good, they want to be remembered, and many will want to be remembered for helping others find a way to get a grip.

An Ace Doesn't Always Look Like an Ace

The thing about aces is that they don't always look like aces. There have been numerous times in my career where I've identified someone as an ace only for them to drop out of the business not long after they started.

The flipside to this is that for all the people you think will be aces, but who don't turn out to be, you'll also find unexpected aces. I can't tell you how many times I've thought someone was going to be just a customer and he or she turned out to be an ace.

Years ago, I met this delightful young man named Cody. After graduating high school, instead of going to college, Cody decided to go into network marketing. Everyone thought he was crazy. Cody was only eighteen, so in addition to getting nonstop negative feedback from people because of his age, he also had a credibility problem. Who would buy a product from a green-behind-the-ears kid?

No one thought Cody would be an ace, but after a few months, he had 2,200 customers in his group. Four years later when Cody was twenty-two, he had been to forty countries, had met some of the top business people in the world, and had helped many others achieve a high level of success.

Not only did Cody turn out to be an ace, he found several other aces that have helped thousands of people make extra income.

Be confident that your aces will surface. Work hard, stick to the main thing, and you will eventually find your aces.

Don't Ignore the Other Cards

If I handed you a deck of fifty-two and said, "Find the four aces as fast as you can," you would quickly sort through the cards to find those aces. You wouldn't concern yourself with the other cards, but in network marketing, all the cards can play a role.

This business is a community business. Every person in it is critical to your success. As you build your business and start looking for your aces, you'll find many people who just want to be customers. As we've already discussed, customers are the lifeblood of your business. You won't have a business if you don't have customers, so rejoice when someone is only looking to buy your product. You'll also find many people who aren't ready to get started yet, or people who say they're an ace, but don't perform like one. Don't get discouraged, and don't ignore your other cards or your customers. You need everyone to be successful. This is just part of the process. Remember, success to some is only what the product offers. To others, it's making several hundred dollars per month.

I thought one of the very first people I signed up would be an ace, but he quickly dropped out of the business. Before he did, he introduced me to a good friend of his named Joe. I got to know Joe and his wife, Sheila. I didn't realize it at the time, but both Joe and Sheila would become top aces for me. Joe and Sheila also signed up their own aces, thereby helping me develop a nice group of aces in no time at all. In this situation, I lost my first card but gained several aces.

Sometimes in a deck of cards, you will find the ace early on, and other times it might be further in the deck. Just keep sorting and talking to new people. An ace will turn up when you least expect it.

Support Your Aces

We've talked before about how one of the greatest advantages to this business is that it's supportive. Your sponsor supports you, your aces support you, and you support your aces. As soon as I find a new ace, I do everything I can to help them find their own aces. I share my time, my tools, and my resources. This business thrives on supporting others. The more you support and help others succeed in this business, the more success you'll have. Make sure that when you have an ace, you do everything in your power to help them succeed. They may ultimately have more success than you. That's okay. That's what makes this business great.

Because aces are busy, you often have to give them an incentive to be an ace. When you first approach potential aces, they might say, "Thanks for the offer, but I don't have the time to do something else." That may be true, but you can ultimately give them more time by helping them build their businesses. Aces deserve to be free of time constraints. Show how you can do that for them.

Time to Get a Grip

Aces can rocket fuel your business. When it comes to finding aces,

1. Find one ace for each of the four legs of your business.
2. Look for aces everywhere, and don't fret when one doesn't work out.
3. Keep an open mind—aces often come from surprising sources.
4. Support those aces by consistently sharing tools and resources with them.

SECTION 3

◦✦◦

Get Serious

CHAPTER 10
You're the CEO, Act Like It

• ◆ •

"Ninety percent of life is attitude."

—Jim Rohn

Network marketing is a collection of CEOs working hard to have success and support each other. While working together is important, as the CEO, you are the leader of your business. You need to act like it.

Your initiative, your drive, your ambition, and your desire to be productive are imperative to your own success as well as to the success of the people you work with directly. You can rely on the confidence of others for a while, but ultimately you must develop your own drive so you can give it to others while they are developing their own.

As the CEO of your business, you must lead. You have to be the one who is forgoing hours of TV to work. You have to be the one who is using the right tools to generate business. You have to be the one who gets creative so others follow your example. You have to be the visionary who motivates others to succeed because you are the leader.

The Buck Stops Here . . . So Do the Excuses

Being a leader means eliminating excuses because guess what? If you are successful in this business, you can take credit for it, and if you're unsuccessful in this business, you can take credit for that, too.

> *If you are successful in this business, you can take credit for it, and if you're unsuccessful in this business, you can take credit for that, too.*

Remember how I told you I always wanted to be six feet tall? I barely even made it to five foot nine. Imagine how different my life would be if I'd programmed myself to believe I could only achieve if I grew to be six feet tall. Right now, I'd have nothing. Instead, I removed the excuse that I was too short to succeed and got to work.

One of my most successful associates is handicapped. When he walks, he throws his left leg forward. It creates an obvious limp. For him, getting around is much more time consuming and difficult than it is for most of the rest of us. This associate is a phenomenal leader. He is a hard worker who does not let obstacles get in his way, and the people who work with him feed off this. He is successful because he refuses to rely on excuses.

If you find yourself making excuses for anything, you are on the wrong path. Look at this chart of common excuses, find the ones you make, and cross them off your list of excuses.

Common Excuses:

The products are too expensive.
My sponsor does not support me.
The company is always changing things.
My town is too small.
My city is too big.
My area is saturated.
No one has ever heard of this company.
I don't know what to say.
I don't know enough people.
People don't like MLM.
The economy is bad.
I'm too busy.
No one has the time to listen to me.
I'm too old.
I'm too young
I'm not educated enough.
I don't like to sell.

Have Confidence

I've found that many of these excuses develop when a person doesn't have enough confidence in themselves to succeed. When people use excuses such as, "I don't have enough money to do that," or, "I don't have enough education to start this," what they're really saying is, "I don't have the confidence to do that."

Don't look for things that might hold you back. Acknowledge potential barriers and then work with what you have. If you really need more education, get more education. In the meantime, do what you can with the education you have and see what happens. The point is, don't let those excuses stop you from doing something you want to do. The only limits on our success are the ones we impose on ourselves.

The only limits on our success are the ones we impose on ourselves.

Make It Happen

Instead of having an excuse, have a reason. True leaders— true CEOs—make things happen without blaming anyone or anything. If you're not meeting a goal, examine why you're not meeting it and adjust your approach. Reasons are not excuses. They are outcomes that can be fixed through action.

Time to Get a Grip

Act like the CEO of your company by:

1. Looking through your list of excuses and committing to eliminating them.
2. Acknowledging potential barriers and finding ways around them.
3. Understanding the reason a certain outcome occurred and then changing your future approach to get a better, clearer outcome.

CHAPTER 11

Accept Who You Are

· ♦ ·

"Your . . . potential . . . is . . . the person you can become."

—John Maxwell

Vietnam taught me dozens of lessons, but the lesson that stands out the most is, *go with what you've got*. Every time we were sent on a mission, we wanted more than what we had. We wanted more artillery support and we wanted more weapons on the nose of the aircraft. Sometimes, we wanted *twice* the number of aircraft that we were given. Sometimes we didn't know the weather report. Other times we knew we weren't going to be able to count on support from other units in the area. That was just the way it was. Every time we went on a mission, we had to go with what we had.

If we'd sat around complaining about what we'd been given, we never would have completed our missions. If I had sat there and said, "I can't go on that mission because I need x, y, and z," we would have gotten nowhere. Lives were on the line, and we had to do the best we could.

Sometimes it's frustrating to try to finish a task when you don't feel you have all the tools you need to complete that task successfully . . . but you know what? Life isn't perfect. Sometimes you have to *go with what you've got.* To succeed in network marketing—to succeed in life—you have to learn to get things done by going with what you've got.

> *To succeed in network marketing—to succeed in life—you have to learn to get things done by going with what you've got.*

Going with what you've got means knowing what your personal strengths and weakness are. What do you currently *have?* What are your best attributes? What differentiates you from everyone else? Maybe you're highly educated. Maybe you're outgoing. Maybe you're well-traveled or articulate. Maybe you're a kind person. Whatever that thing is, embrace it because people will buy from and do business with people they know and trust. They will trust you when you are confident in who you are. Don't try to be something different. You can be you.

In this business, *who* you are matters. Be comfortable with you, and if there's anything you don't like about being you, know that only you have the power to change it.

Accept Who You Are

The most successful people I know understand their strengths *and* weaknesses. They recognize their strengths so they can capitalize on them and share them with others. They know their weaknesses so they can grow out of them, improve upon them, or find team members who can help fill the gap those weaknesses leave.

To keep on top of both your strengths and weaknesses, constantly check in with yourself. Ask yourself questions such as:

1. What are my strengths?
2. What are my weaknesses?
3. What do I admire in others?
4. What do I spend the majority of my time doing?
5. Am I dependable?
6. Do I smile and laugh?
7. Would I do business with myself?

The answers to these questions define you. They help you see what there is to like about yourself (your strengths) and what you might need to improve upon (your weaknesses).

Even if you want to change a few things about who you are, honor yourself the way you are today. Don't be afraid to be who you are. Love and appreciate yourself. You'll see that when you start believing in yourself, you'll become unstoppable. You must be happy with who you are before you can really start making changes that will lead to a better life and the ability to help more people.

Change the Things You Want to Change

One of the greatest benefits to this industry is personal development. Network marketing provides so many opportunities to learn from others, which is incredible because it allows you to change and evolve while honoring who you are already.

I've always loved talking to people and enjoyed inviting them to do things. That's who I am, it's what I'm good at. When I first went into network marketing, I thought that if a person I'd invited to an event or presentation said they'd show, they'd show up. I was wrong. I can't tell you how many times I've waited around for no shows, wondering why they didn't show. A yes is a yes, right? Wrong. I used to get very frustrated when they didn't show up. I soon realized that people often say yes to be nice. So, I changed my tactic. I didn't change the way I talked to people—I did that well and didn't want to change who I was. Instead, I changed how I approached my attitude toward invites. Instead of assuming people would show up the first time, I started asking if I could come to them.

After a long day of work, after being stuck in traffic, very few people want to come to *you* to hear a presentation. However, many people don't mind if you come to them or offer to take them out to a meal or coffee to hear your presentation. Also, I have found that regular weekly meetings are more effective now as a second look. Instead of inviting people to a meeting where they had very little information about what was going to be discussed, I've found that if I've already had a chance to talk to them about my product or business, they are much more likely to show up to get more information. They have a reason to come.

For this example, I honored who I was while changing a small thing in my process that would lead to better outcomes. You can do this, too. First, in addition to asking questions about who you are, like we talked about earlier, ask questions about who you *want* to be. Do you want to be attractive to others by your actions, words, the way you carry yourself, and the way you relate to other people? What is your plan for growth? How do the answers to these questions make up your personal philosophy?

Your personal philosophy will determine where you are headed and whether others will want to go there with you. If you want to be more outgoing, caring, compassionate, or encouraging, you can do that. Our traits can be modified. Sometimes they can be modified too easily, sometimes they're modified to our benefit, and other times they're modified to our detriment. If you don't like where you are today, change it.

I know a married couple from Iowa that put four girls through college by selling dresses at a retail store. After count-less years of hard work in that industry, they looked at their life, decided they didn't like the gains they received for all that work, and changed to network marketing.

I have seen a PhD in physics change to network marketing just like I've seen stay-at-home parents, accountants, unemployed individuals, and attorneys become successful in this marvelous industry simply by agreeing to and committing to making a change. You can change your life for the better if you want to.

Think about it like this. Ronald Reagan first ran for public office when he was fifty-five. Colonel Sanders started Kentucky Fried Chicken when he was sixty-five. It's never too late to start a new endeavor or business. It's never too late to make a change.

To say you cannot teach an old dog new tricks might be accurate for a dog, but it's just not so for humans. An attitude of learning, growing, and developing is ours for the taking throughout our lives.

> *To say you cannot teach an old dog new tricks might be accurate for a dog, but it's just not so for humans.*

Don't be Afraid of Being Abnormal

We're into chapter eleven of *Get A Grip* and you're still reading. To me, that says you're abnormal. To be normal means to accept the rut. To be abnormal is to do something about it.

Abnormal means you have ambition, which is admirable. You are willing to work hard, you want to improve the world, and you want to lead a significant life. You are willing to take risks. You believe that it's better to have loved and lost than to have never loved at all.

I like being abnormal. Why? Because normal has many weaknesses. They include:

Early morning alarms

Fighting traffic to work

Meeting with bosses you dislike

Challenges with coworkers

Unreasonable deadlines

Taking work home

Begging for raises

Begging for vacation time

Having unfulfilling days

Not having enough money at the end of every month

I like being abnormal because I don't have any of those problems. Instead I:

Stay in bed until I'm through sleeping

Work at home

Work with whom I wish

Spend time with family

Go on fun vacations frequently

Work for myself

Pay off debt

I love being abnormal because it means I have a grip. I am unwilling to accept the rut that most are willing to stay mired in. I never want to be part of the majority who never break free of the bondage required to keep their head above water. I don't want to retire unable to meet my financial needs, spending every day worrying that my money will run out before I'm ready for it to. If you're ready to get a grip, you need to accept that there's a part of you that's a little abnormal. Accept it and then protect it.

The Chicken or the Egg?

One of the most interesting things about changing certain actions or characteristics about yourself is that sometimes you have success before you make the change. It sounds counterintuitive, but it's true.

There was a wonderful person in my life who didn't think he could make it in network marketing because he was so shy. Of course, I wanted him to make it so I told him, "You really need to work on being more outgoing. You really need to make an effort to look people in the eyes when you speak to them."

For him, that was much easier said than done; however, once he started having a small amount of success, he was more confident, which led to even more success. So sometimes we need the courage to go with what we have until we have a little success to boost our confidence. Then, we can work on those things we really want to improve.

Time to Get a Grip

Become a better you by:

1. Really getting to know yourself by asking the questions outlined in this chapter.
2. Loving yourself as you are and gradually making changes to improve the things you want to change.
3. Knowing not only who you are, but who you want to be and working toward becoming that person.
4. Not being afraid of being abnormal.

SECTION 4

· ◆ ·

Get Methodical

CHAPTER 12

Sales? What's That?

• ◆ •

"Great leaders have ambition beyond their own personal self-interest."

—Jim Collins

Some people in this industry will say that they are not in the business of selling, or that they are not in network marketing at all. I believe that's not true.

The truth is, those of us in this business *are* salespeople. We *are* network marketers. Why not be proud of that? After all, this is a great profession. Through sales, network marketing provides the fairest business model for anyone who is willing to work hard to develop a business that will give himself the freedom to enjoy his life. I love it because it gives those who work consistently the opportunity to create extra monthly income so they can achieve financial freedom. We give people hope, we give them freedom, and we give them opportunities and we do it all through selling.

Some people prefer to think of selling and network marketing as sharing or educating. Of course, sales and network marketing are sharing and educating. I wouldn't love this industry so much or have stayed with it for so long if it weren't about sharing and educating people about a new product or business. However, success only comes if you exchange a product or service for money. If your product or service is valuable, if the exchange is fair and you can demonstrate that, you make a sale.

For some people, the term selling carries with it negative associations. They think of it as a pushy way to get people to buy a product. Don't think of it that way. I see selling as a way to constantly influence people toward making the decisions that will have the greatest positive impact on their lives. I am confident in my abilities to sell, and I am proud of my ability to sell and in this industry. I want you to feel the same.

Selling is not a negative. It's a positive opportunity to help people improve their lives.

Get comfortable with the term selling because that's what you, as the CEO of your own company, will be doing. Yes, you'll share and educate, but at the end of the day, to have success, you'll have to sell. As far as I know, there has never been a vice president of sharing in any company, but there are thousands of vice presidents of sales. There's a reason for that.

We can all sell with integrity and honesty by doing these five things:

1. Engaging people
2. Knowing a product's features and benefits
3. Using testimonials and other validation
4. Countering objections
5. Developing a strong close

Your company likely has tools that will help you with several of these steps. You'll certainly want to use their tools. The more proficient you become with these steps, the more effective you will become.

Time to Get a Grip

Get familiar and excited about who you are. Remember that:

1. Selling is a wonderful opportunity to influence people to make decisions that will improve their lives.
2. You can help improve the lives of your customers by engaging them, knowing a product's features and benefits, using testimonials, countering objections, and developing a strong close.

CHAPTER 13
Get Engaged

• ◆ •

*"Influence other people.
Talk about what they want and
show them how to get it."*

—Dale Carnegie

Many in this industry think the gift of gab is the most important requirement for success. They often point to the three-foot rule—if someone is within three feet of you, engage them in conversation—as proof of that. I tend to agree, but I also think there is some skill involved in talking to people. If you immediately start talking to a potential customer about your product or opportunity, their defense wall will go up. This won't help you.

The absolute best way to get someone interested in what you have to say is to engage *them* first. Focus your conversation on the person and wait for them to show interest or ask you what to do before telling them anything about your company, product, or business opportunity. What's important to them? What makes them tick? Where do they want their lives to go?

The absolute best way to get someone interested in
what you have to say is to engage them first.

Small talk demonstrates that you care for your prospect and his or her concerns. After the small talk, after you demonstrate interest in the other person, then you can start talking about yourself and your product. This takes practice. It also takes authenticity. Don't just *act* like you care about the people you're talking to, genuinely care. Sometimes you will have conversations with people and your business or product may never come up. That's okay. If you always have an agenda, people will be able to tell. Instead, enjoy meeting new people. When you care about them, they will care about what you do.

How to Start the Conversation

As with all skills, starting conversations is easier for some people than it is for others. Whether you find starting conversations easy or hard, a good rule of thumb for starting quality conversations that will focus on the other person is FORM.

Questions for meeting new people:

Family:

- Where do you live
- Where did you grow up?
- Do you have any kids?
- Is everyone in your family healthy?

Occupation:

- What do you do?
- Do you enjoy your job?
- Do you like going to work every day?
- If you did what you really wanted to do, what would that be?

Recreation:

- Have you seen any good movies lately?
- What do you like to do for fun?
- Do you work out?
- Have you been on a fun vacation lately?
- What makes you tick? (one of my favorites)

Money:

- What is your plan for retirement?
- Does your company give you a raise very often?
- Have you ever owned your own business?
- Have you ever thought about creating an extra stream of income?

Asking someone questions about family, occupation, recreation, or money will inevitably get a good conversation going without focusing on your product or business.

FORM helps you find out what's important to prospects: what they like to do, where they're satisfied and dissatisfied with their life, or how happy they are with their jobs. Ask FORM questions and then ask for details. If prospects have a desire to improve their lives, ask them where specifically they'd like to improve.

As Theodore Roosevelt said, "Nobody cares how much you know, until they know how much you care." This is why your questions have to reflect how much you really care about others. They must be genuine.

Tell a Great Story

When it's time to transition from listening to talking, tell stories that capture their imagination. Tell stories that are relevant to them. Talk about the successes you or others have had so the listener feels inspired to dream again. Help them see how your vehicle (your product and business) can carry them to great places.

I loved AT&T's reach out and touch someone campaign because it demonstrates this perfectly. That motto means that by talking to someone, we are participating in their lives. We are involved, and we are affecting them through our words and actions.

When you talk to people, always have a brochure you can leave with them or a website to send them to. Check in with them while you're talking to make sure they're still engaged and make sure to set an appointment to tell them more . . . and then follow up on that agreement.

Time to Get a Grip

To engage your customers:

1. Get to know them first. What's important to them? What makes them tick? Where do they want their lives to go?
2. Don't just *act* like you care about clients, genuinely care and don't be bothered if your product never comes up in conversation.
3. Start a quality conversation that focuses on FORM (family, occupation, recreation, money).
4. Tell a great story.

CHAPTER 14
Know Your Product, Be a Benefit

• ♦ •

"Make your prospects curious."

—Eric Worre

There are thousands of different companies with thousands of different products and compensation plans, yet each has something that makes it unique. You need to know what makes your product unique. You don't have to be a product expert, but you do need to know what product literature or other tools you have at your disposal to help make your product stand out in the marketplace.

You need to know your product's benefits, and then you need to promote those benefits because the product—and ultimately your ability to convey that information—is the key indicator of your future success.

Capture Your Audience's Imagination

To get prospects interested in your product or business, you first have to capture their imagination. Say something that is valuable to them, something that gets them thinking about how your product could benefit them and their loved ones.

Capturing someone's imagination really gets him or her interested in your product. For example, one time I was speaking to a woman named Deborah. I found out she was a brand-new mom. She also was very successful in the advertising business but really didn't want to go back to work. Her husband made a good income, but they needed a little more money each month to pay their bills. This was a perfect opportunity to talk to Deborah about starting a network marketing business. I told her that if she was willing to put in a few hours a week, I would help her make enough money to pay those bills. She ended up being very gung ho and did well in this business. What would have happened if I hadn't captured her imagination? What if I just started telling her about something she wasn't interested in? I found out what she was concerned about, and then I captured her imagination.

Remember, every person you speak with has to see how your product or business has the potential to change his or her life. Capture prospects' imagination by showing how the product has the potential to *help* them.

> *Remember, every person you speak with has to see how your product has the potential to change his or her lives.*

Develop Your Initial Benefit Statement

To capture your audience's imagination, develop a strong initial benefit statement or initial benefit question that is relevant to them. This statement or question will immediately resonate with that person. It will make them think, "That's exactly what I need to fix problem x," and make them curious to know more.

There are many different network marketing products. Many offer a solution around feeling better, looking better, or getting in better shape. Products also offer legal services, energy services, items for the home, and more.

Below are some of the questions I've asked to capture someone's imagination:

How would you like to *feel great every day?*
How would you like to *have more energy?*
How would you like to *improve your memory?*
How would you like to *be in the best shape of your life?*
How would you like to *have great-looking skin?*
How would you like to *own your own business?*
How would you like to *make an extra stream of income?*
How would you like to *pay off your debt?*
How would you like to *own your own life?*
How would you like to *earn your living working from home?*
How would you like to *set your own hours?*
How would you like to *feel secure with your retirement planning?*

These are great suggestions, but find what works for you and your product.

Once you know the client's needs, you can offer an initial benefit statement. An initial benefit statement might look like this:

I can show you *a way to consume much better nutrition.*

I can show you how to *have the best health possible.*

I can show you how to *be in the best shape of your life.*

I can show you how to *have more energy every day.*

I can show you how to *have more time with those you love.*

I can show you how to *be debt free.*

I can show you how to *travel the world.*

I can show you how to *dream big again.*

I can show you how to *own your own business.*

I can show you how to *have money left over at the end of every month.*

I can show you how to *improve your retirement.*

I can show you how to *have a better attitude and grow as a person.*

Our business can answer many of the prayers that your prospects may have. It's your job to find out what they are worried about or what their interests are.

Some Imaginations Won't Be Captured

One quote I just love is, "It's difficult to say the right thing to the wrong person or the wrong thing to the right person."

While you run into plenty of people like Deborah who will show great interest in you, your product, or your business, you'll also run into people who—no matter what you say—simply won't be interested. These are the wrong people. They're the people who no matter how much you explain the benefits of entrepreneurship, won't be interested right now.

That's okay. Maybe they'll be interested in the future. You never know; life happens. On the flip side, they may never be interested. That's okay, too. The good news is that there will always be more people who will be very interested. You just have to find them and capture their imaginations.

Time to Get a Grip

Get your prospect interested in your product or business by:

1. Knowing what makes your product unique and using the literature and other tools you have at your disposal to help make your product stand out in the marketplace.

2. Capturing your prospect's imagination by showing how your product or business has the potential to *help* him or her.

3. Developing an initial benefit statement that says exactly how your product will solve that particular prospect's need.

CHAPTER 15

No Thank You?
Yes Please

• ♦ •

"Every adversity brings with it the seed of an equivalent advantage."

—Napoleon Hill

Rejection is really tough for most people to handle because it doesn't feel good. People take rejection personally because it *feels* personal. However, when someone rejects an offer, they're not rejecting the person making the offer.

I've been doing this for decades and can tell you the four most common reasons people say no are:

1. It's not the right time.
2. They don't understand the product's benefit.
3. They don't feel they have enough information to buy.
4. They are too distracted by life to listen properly.

——— ♦ ———

People don't reject you because they don't like you, think your presentation was bad, or think you're a bad person. Why? *Because in most cases, rejections are not personal.* Do not take them personally. Rejection is part of business.

Your job is to give people information. Some will give you a no in return and some will give you a yes. Both are okay. As a matter of fact, some nos become yeses later, so keep good relationships with people.

"No" Is One Step Closer to the Next "Yes"

I have a bold attitude toward nos that comes from the Bible. The Bible says that if I share salvation with someone and it isn't accepted, I can wipe the dust off my sandals and tell someone else. That's pretty bold. The best product I can ever offer is salvation. So, if I'm allowed to be bold in that regard, then why can't I apply that same attitude toward selling my product or service? When I get a no, I respect the answer and then go ask someone else.

As you go out there every day sharing information with others, keep in mind that every no gets you one step closer to the next yes. When you share information that can improve someone's life, you bear information that can help them. If they say no, it's their loss, but it's also their choice. People have a right to decide what's best for them. Do not take their initial no personally.

I'm never upset with a no. I know there are reasons beyond my control for those nos and that the more I get, the closer I am to a yes. The only time I get upset with a no is when I know I've gotten a no because I've tried to close too soon. I'll talk more about closing in chapter sixteen.

If you find yourself feeling down about a no, remember this: Every year, many networking companies host incentive trips for the most successful people in their business. Guess who never shows up? The people who never closed because they were afraid of getting a no. When I'm on one of those trips, I congratulate the people who earned the incentive trip for first saying yes themselves, and then for accepting nos from others so they could get more yeses.

Be Okay with Mistakes

As you accept each no to get closer to those yeses, you will make some mistakes. Maybe you closed too early, didn't capture the person's imagination, or failed to engage him or her in the right way. That's okay. We all make mistakes.

In fact, name a great basketball player who's never fouled, a great skier who has never fallen, or a great pianist who has never hit the wrong key. Can't think of anyone? Of course not. Practice minimizes mistakes, but even people who are at the top of their game make mistakes. Expect mistakes, and don't be too hard on yourself when you make them.

*Practice minimizes mistakes, but even people
who are at the top of their game make mistakes.
Expect mistakes, and don't be too hard on
yourself when you make them.*

Accepting that we will frequently make mistakes keeps us from feeling foolish, which is an immobilizing feeling. A fear of messing up our image causes inaction. The best way to keep from making a mistake is to do nothing. And the best way to ensure dynamic lack of success is to do nothing.

Being no-free and mistake-free will make you success-free. Accept nos and mistakes.

Learn from them and move on. Be delighted that you are putting a foot forward, that you are active. If a foot gets stepped on, take a step backward to evaluate what happened and step forward again with a new tactic or new direction. Remember, those who expect perfection from themselves or others will always come up short. They will never get a grip.

*Being no-free and mistake-free will make
you success-free.*

Prepare for Common Objections

The great thing about this industry is that it allows you to constantly learn and change your approach. Through this process, you will have the opportunity to hear common objections and head them off at the pass.

One of the most common objections is, "I can't afford that right now."

I am always ready for that objection. Usually, the prospect will say something like, "I don't know where I'm going to find an extra $100 a month in my budget."

I love when people come back with this because it's an easy objection to walk them through. I simply tell them where they might save an extra $100 a month. Maybe instead of buying coffee at a café, they make their coffee at home. Or maybe they stop eating breakfast out for just one month and it saves them $170.

Also, find out if your company offers a product guarantee. That often helps.

I tell them I will help them get started and that I will help them with their referrals. I am always ready to show a new person what they need to do to earn enough money to pay for their own monthly costs. Do this correctly and at some point, the only logical response to your questions is yes.

A few other common objections in this industry are:

1. I don't want to get involved in a pyramid scheme.
2. Only the people at the top make money.
3. The commission structure just drives up the price.

Here's how I address each:

I don't want to get involved in a pyramid scheme.

In network marketing, people work together as a team to sell products and then share in the commissions from those products.

Sometimes a network marketing business is demonstrated by drawing circles in the SHAPE of a pyramid. This puts you at the top, and you sell products to customers and distributors, who sell more products to customers and other distributors as the pyramid broadens. Because there is more volume on each level, the model takes on a pyramid shape.

In reality, network marketing doesn't look like a pyramid. Sometimes you have more volume on the first level than you do on the level below that. Other times, your business looks more like a pear and so on. That being said, there is nothing wrong with a business that is shaped like a pyramid. Think about the organizational chart of the company you currently work for. What shape is it? A pyramid. What about the organizational chart of the military or your family tree? Both are pyramids.

While there's nothing wrong with a pyramid shape, not all network marketing companies are created equal. The business model itself has been long established, but because the network marketing industry is growing fast, there are always individuals who might start companies with the wrong motivations, substandard products, or lack of focus on staying within legal boundaries. That is why it is so important to choose the *right* company to build your business with.

Only the people at the top make money.

Think about your job. If you work at a large corporation, or even a smaller business, the people who started that business or the top executives make most of the money. The people at the bottom—the workers—earn a very small percentage of the overall payroll. In many network marketing plans, the closer you are to the volume, the higher percentage you will earn. This feature allows the people who are the most productive to make the most money. That's the way it should be. I know of many top money earners in this industry who didn't start out when their company started. They joined the company years after the company launched but, because they were productive and created a lot of volume, they had the opportunity to earn the most money.

One of the best things about network marketing is that it doesn't matter when or where you start. The opportunity is the same. In other industries, if someone doesn't have the right background, education, or connections, the chance of becoming CEO is almost zero. If that same person starts a network marketing business, the only thing that matters is volume and developing aces. If this person speaks to enough people, sells enough product, and gets enough distributors to sell product, he or she can rise to be one of the top income earners in any company. To me, that makes network marketing one of the fairest industries in the world.

The commission structure just drives up the price.

As with products in every industry, some network marketing companies sell overpriced products, but that has nothing to do with the pay plan.

As we discussed in chapter five, instead of paying one person 30 percent for a commission, the company will stretch that same commission over multiple levels so a 30 percent commission might be stretched out at 5 percent over six levels. This creates that opportunity for leverage. Instead of only being paid on your own efforts, you can be paid on the efforts of many others.

Most products that are sold by a retail distribution model, such as tennis shoes, coffee, makeup, or nutritional products, have to factor in many layers of middlemen and advertising costs. Often, the advertising by itself represents 40 to 50 percent of the cost of the product.

I find that when I walk through the answers to these common objections, people are much more receptive to what I have to say. I'm so used to objections that I welcome them. They give me an opportunity to get into further detail about my product and how that product might help whomever I'm talking to. Listen to your common objections, develop realistic responses to them, and help more people.

No Today Isn't No Tomorrow.

The last point I want to make about objections is that usually when people say no, they mean not today. Today, they may not be in a place in that moment where they want to change their life. That's okay.

Many of today's nos will turn into yeses later if you don't burn your bridges. I have had people call me long after they told me no to ask if I could show them my program again. As I mentioned before, people say no for many reasons. You never know what that reason is or when they may change their mind.

If I get a no today and I can tell I need to let that person go, I set up another appointment with them so I can revisit the topic on a day that they might be a yes. I can't tell you how many times I've done this and worked with a person—sometimes for years—before they become a yes.

Let rejections roll off your back, take the ones off the table that you can, and be patient.

Time to Get a Grip

Learn to take rejections on the chin by:

1. Understanding they are not personal.
   They are not about you.
2. Accepting that every no gets you one step closer to a yes.
3. Understand that there's a reason people say no.
   Figure out what it is and how you can improve your
   pitch to get rid of those future nos.
4. Heading common objections off at the pass.
5. Knowing that a no today is not a no tomorrow.

CHAPTER 16
Learn to Close

• ◆ •

"Get your ask in gear!"

—Rita Davenport

For many people, closing is really difficult. They don't have any issues with starting a conversation, setting up an appointment, talking about the value of their product, or sharing features and benefits, but they come up short when it's time to ask for the sale.

Part of the reason for this is that they flat out haven't practiced their closing techniques enough. In the beginning, your enthusiasm is all you will need to be successful, but over time, you'll need to develop these skills we'll talk about in this chapter to keep closing well. To become good at closing, you need a lot of practice and a lot of experience. Luckily, you don't have to do it all yourself. Your company may have tools that can help, but tools can't do everything for you. If you don't have any experience with closing, get help from your sponsor or someone in your group that is good at closing. Closing is a skill that *can* be learned and developed over time if you have the right attitude.

Master Your Trial Close

When you get a rejection like we talked about in chapter fifteen, congratulate yourself on completing a *trial close*. A trial close is nothing more than practice close. We need to go through these because practice makes perfect. The more you try for a yes, the closer you get to one, but in the meantime, you're going to get some nos. Don't worry, you'll get plenty of yeses, too.

When you walk away from a trial close, always assess what you could have done to turn that trial into an actual close. Often, the person simply wasn't ready to buy—it wasn't the right time—and other times you can learn from mistakes that might have brought them to yes that day. Maybe you need to know more about your product, present its benefits differently, or do more research on that product.

If you try to close and then get an objection like we discussed in chapter fifteen, be prepared and then calmly answer the objection. If you don't know the answer, it's okay to say, "I'll find that out for you." Keep in mind that most objections are related to one of the objections we've already covered. When the objection is raised, don't get defensive. Instead, confidently answer the concern.

When you get a trial close, you must probe to find out additional information is necessary so you can close again. Ask the prospect a question that will lead to a yes answer. These questions might include:

1. Would you like to start with this product or that product?
2. Would you prefer to pay by check or credit card?
3. Can you attend a training at my house this Saturday or would next week be better?

After probing, answer the questions and objections that prospect might have while they still feel cautious and unsure and ask to plan a specific follow-up appointment.

A trial close is never wasted. It's simply one step to your close.

You Get What You Ask For

The best way to ask for a sale is to recap the features and benefits of the product by asking the client a few questions. For example, if you're selling a health product, you might say:

1. Do you think your current diet is providing all the nutrition necessary for the best health?
2. Do you have a plan for improvement?
3. Do you think this quality product could be beneficial?

Try the same tactic when asking someone if they're interested in a business opportunity. Start by asking a few of the following questions:

1. Are you satisfied with your current financial position?
2. Do you have a plan to improve?
3. Would you be interested in earning some extra income?
4. Are you aware of how network marketing works?

These questions plant a seed in prospects' minds. It gets them thinking about a problem so you can present the solution.

Assume the Answer Is Yes

Always go into a sale assuming they will say yes. Know your presentation is great and go in with confidence because your prospect will feel that confidence. If you radiate confidence, it will greatly affect your outcome. Confidence sends a strong, affirmative message to your prospect that they need to buy. Of course they are going to get started! Of course they are going to buy your product! If you are confident, they want to do that before you say anything.

I can't tell you how many people tell me I'm good at closing because I'm a natural. That isn't true. I'm good at closing because I have the right attitude about closing. As with everything in this business, closing is 95 percent attitude. If you think you can close, you will close.

> *As with everything in this business,*
> *closing is 95 percent attitude.*
> *If you think you can close,*
> *you will close.*

Stop assuming the worst-case scenario and start assuming the best case. If your prospects have objections, they will tell you. Be ready for it, but also be ready for them to say yes.

To make that yes a reality, I do the following before I close:

I show up with gifts, samples of the product, or other items that prospects can take home.

I know how well my products work.

I know my prospects will thank me later after they experience good results.

Closing can be fun. If after reading this you still feel unsure about closing, bring someone who is more confident closing along and let them do their magic. Like I've said before, one of the benefits to this industry is that we all work together. If you do better, I do better so if you need help, just ask. You will soon be closing like a pro!

Time to Get a Grip

Master your close by:

1. Assuming every sale will be a yes.
2. Exuding confidence.
3. Knowing your product's benefits and features.
4. Having the right attitude about closing.

CONCLUSION: Get Going

• ◆ •

"What lies behind us and what lies before us are tiny matters compared to what lies within us."

—Ralph Waldo Emerson

I had a Harley-Davidson motorcycle in college that only had a kick-start capability. I often wondered why it would start easily one day and then need a dozen kicks the next day to get going.

I started keeping statistics to determine whether there were scientific reasons for the difference in how many kicks (how much effort) was required. I kept charts on the time of day, the temperature, the time since last used, the amount of fuel in the tank, the last time I took a pretty girl for a ride, what my attitude was, and others.

I finally determined that there was no scientific reason for the number of kicks required to start a Harley-Davidson motorcycle. While this might not be the answer I'd hoped for, there is a philosophical lesson to be learned from this experiment: it doesn't matter how long you have to kick something to get it to go. If you don't kick it until it starts, you won't go for a ride!

Now that you've taken the time to survey your current situation, realistically weigh the pros and cons in your life, and look at the things that need changing, congratulate yourself! You've taken the first step toward investing the time and energy you need to get a grip. You've given network marketing its first kick. You have given yourself the opportunity to take control of your finances, enjoy your job, and set yourself free. You have given yourself a chance to *change your life.*

Of course, this won't happen without a little work. Like any other business, to succeed in network marketing, you must commit to working hard. You must get gung ho! You need to commit to persistence, and you have to commit to the time and energy that will drive your outcomes. The key is to keep kicking. Don't quit. It won't be easy, but it will be worthwhile.

The great thing about network marketing is that it offers a few things other industries do not. It offers you the opportunity to make your own hours, control your own outcomes, start a business with minimal upfront money, and change your life. After working in multiple industries and starting several other businesses, I can tell you that this is a blessing. Not only does network marketing give you an unprecedented chance to be the CEO of your own company, it's structured in such a way that when one person does well, everyone does well. I challenge you to find any other industry where every single person delights in the success of the people around them.

I came to network marketing not because I had to, but because I wanted to. I understood the financial opportunity it could provide for the people around me. As long as you are committed to working hard, and as long as you choose the right network marketing company and understand the simple equation "Product value = more customers = more income," you will succeed in this industry.

Whether you're interested in network marketing as a full-time career or a part-time income boost, know that you have everything you need within you to succeed. You can do it, and you will do it because you've taken the first step toward:

- Programming yourself for success.
- Understanding what it means to be the CEO of your own company.
- Finding the four aces that will accelerate your business.
- Working with the equation that product value = more customers.
- Employing sales tactics that will work for you and your customers.

I can't tell you how excited I am to know that you're ready to start changing your life. There is nothing better than committing to help yourself because once you do that, you'll be able to help others. Take the tools outlined in Get a Grip, get gung ho about network marketing, and take control of your future today.

Ray Robbins

Your Get a Grip Action Plan

62 Network Marketing Tips That Will Change Your Life

Section 1: Get Uplifted

Chapter 1: Believe in This Business

Eliminate any misconceptions you have about network marketing and understand that it:

1. Is the only industry that lets you build your own business, be your own boss, and control your own income.

2. Has been endorsed by business leaders and economists all over the world.

3. Will change your life by letting you earn more money than any other industry, immediately improving your quality of life and putting your earning potential into your hands.

4. Lets you create recurring income with very little investment.

Chapter 2: Believe in Yourself

Program yourself for success today by:

5. Taking a close look at the conversations you have with yourself and how the emotional elements of those conversations project to the world.
6. Give yourself an attitude check. Consider how you approach successes and failures and commit to approaching both with a positive attitude.
7. Delight in the success of others.
8. Surround yourself with positive people who are projecting what you want from your own life.

Chapter 3: Retire with Network Marketing

Want to retire through network marketing? Ask yourself the following:

9. At my current salary level and savings rate, how long will it take for me to save enough money to retire?
10. How would generating $1,000 to $3,000 a month help myself and my family? What stress would it relieve?
11. What activities can I reduce or stop altogether (watching TV, social media) that would free up more time for me to pursue this idea of creating recurring income for myself?
12. How can I develop a plan today to make more money than I spend?

Section 2: Get Started

Chapter 4: Get Started

To get started in network marketing, understand that:

13. The minimal sacrifices you make today have the potential to drastically change your life ten years from now.
14. No other business model allows its owners to start with such a small investment.
15. Even if you only want to work in network marketing five to ten hours a week, you must commit to those five to ten hours.
16. Like every other business out there, your approach to network marketing must be methodical.

Chapter 5: Pick a Company

When you start looking at product, consider the following:

17. Is the company selling a sustainable product?
18. Does the company have a seamless compensation plan?
19. Is the product proprietary?
20. Is the product something I can personally get excited about?
21. What percentage of people who buy the product buy it as customers only?

Chapter 6: Develop Your Plan

Network marketing is great because it allows you to determine your life's purpose. Do that by:

22. Asking yourself, "Why am I going to stick with this business when someone tells me no?"
23. Developing a long-term goal that has nothing to do with financial outcomes.
24. Looking at your long-term goals and deciding where you want to be in the next year, five years, and ten years.
25. Building short-term goals that include specific actions that will help you reach those long-term outcomes.
26. Writing your goals in pencil and sharing them with your team.

Chapter 7: Use Your Tools

Effectively use your tools by:

27. Finding the tools that work the best for you.
28. Ensuring that you don't get so wrapped up in exploring various tools that you stop doing the main thing, which is building volume.
29. Being open to trying new tools, especially as they experience technological changes.

Chapter 8: Never Quit

Anyone who has started a business knows that at some point, you'll feel like giving up. The successful ones don't. When you feel like quitting:

30. Know that to succeed in every industry, you must persist.
31. Be patient. There isn't a single successful businessman or businesswoman who made a fortune the day they opened their business.
32. Focus on the activities and actions that have the greatest potential to grow your business.
33. Commit to never giving up, and you will succeed.

Chapter 9: Find Your Aces

Aces can rocket your business. When it comes to finding aces:

34. Find one ace for each of the four legs of your business.
35. Look for aces everywhere, and don't fret when one doesn't work out.
36. Keep an open mind—aces often come from surprising sources.
37. Support those aces by consistently sharing tools and resources with them.

Section 3: Get Serious

Chapter 10: You're the CEO, Act Like It
Act like the CEO of your company by:

38. Looking through your list of excuses and committing to eliminating them.
39. Acknowledging potential barriers and finding ways around them.
40. Understanding the reason a certain outcome occurred and then changing your future approach to get a better, clearer outcome.

Chapter 11: Accept Who You Are
Become a better you by:

41. Really getting to know yourself by asking the questions outlined in this chapter.
42. Loving yourself as you are and gradually making changes to improve the things you want to change.
43. Knowing not only who you are, but who you want to be and working toward becoming that person.
44. Not being afraid of being abnormal.

Section 4: Get Methodical

Chapter 12: Sales? What's That?

Get familiar and excited about who you are. Remember:

45. Selling is a wonderful opportunity to influence people to make decisions that will improve their lives.
46. You can help improve the lives of your customers by engaging them, knowing a product's features and benefits, using testimonials, countering objectives, and developing a strong close.

Chapter 13: Get Engaged

To engage your customers:

47. Get to know them first. What's important to them? What makes them tick? Where do they want their lives to go?
48. Don't just *act* like you care about clients, genuinely care and don't be bothered if your product never comes up in conversation.
49. Start a quality conversation that focuses on FORM (family, occupation, recreation, money).
50. Tell a great story.

Chapter 14: Know Your Product, Be a Benefit

Get your prospect interested in your product by:

51. Knowing what makes your product unique and using the literature and other tools you have at your disposal to help make your product stand out in the marketplace.

52. Capturing your prospect's imagination by showing how your product or business has the potential to *help* him or her.

53. Developing an initial benefit statement that says exactly how your product will solve that particular prospect's need.

Chapter 15: No Thank You? Yes Please

Learn to take rejections on the chin by:

54. Understanding they are not personal. They are not about you.

55. Accepting that every no gets you one step closer to a yes.

56. Understand that there's a reason people say no. Figure out what it is and how you can improve your pitch to get rid of those future nos.

57. Heading common objections off at the pass.

58. Knowing that a no today is not a no tomorrow.

Chapter 16: Learn to Close

Master your close by:

59. Assuming every sale will be a yes.
60. Exuding confidence.
61. Knowing your product's benefits and features.
62. Having the right attitude about closing.

ABOUT THE AUTHORS

♦

About Ray Robbins

After starting and running multiple successful businesses, Ray Robbins decided to pursue network marketing, an industry that has captured his heart, full-time. For more than forty years, Ray has found personal and financial freedom through the network marketing industry where he earns more than $2 million annually.

Ray is among the top ten income earners of all time in the network marketing industry. He has served on the board of a publicly traded company, a privately held company, a large school district, and a bank. He has also owned many private businesses.

Before starting a career in business, Ray received his bachelors of science in Biology and Chemistry from Southwest Texas State University. Ray also served with the US military for thirteen years. He is a Vietnam veteran, Major, and recipient of the Air Medal, Bronze Star, Army Commendation, National Defense Medal, and Vietnam Campaign and Service Medal.

Ray is well-known among friends and family for his family-first philosophy, which maintains that everyone within his circle is cared for. Ray delights in spending time with his immediate family, which includes wife, Dianna, children Kevin, Ryan, and Marla, and his seven grandkids. Family vacations are a priority for the Robbins family, and Ray loves booking exotic, whirlwind trips.

About Kevin Robbins

Kevin Robbins is a renowned speaker, trainer, and network marketing field leader. Kevin received a bachelor of business administration in marketing at the University of Texas at Arlington. After a successful career in corporate America, Kevin started network marketing part-time in 1994. By 2000, not only was Kevin network marketing full-time, he also had numerous successes in network marketing leadership roles. He currently serves on the board of directors for a publicly traded network marketing company.

Within his company, Kevin has been recognized as a top 100 income earner every year since 1997. He was recognized as part of the Million Dollar Club in 2005. In 2012, Kevin was recognized as one of the Top Global Business Builders of the Year.

Kevin met his wife, Dawn, through a network marketing incentive. They have two wonderful kids, Jordan and Ashlyn. Kevin and Dawn are grateful that network marketing allowed them to both be stay at home parents for their kids as they were growing up.